empowering teenagers through God's grace

the winning spirit

Flagship church resources

from Group Publishing

Innovations From Leading Churches

Flagship Church Resources are your shortcut to innovative and effective leadership ideas. You'll find ideas for every area of church leadership including pastoral ministry, adult ministry, youth ministry, and children's ministry.

Flagship Church Resources are created by the leaders of thriving, dynamic, and trend-setting churches around the country. These nationally recognized teaching churches host regional leadership conferences and are respected by other pastors and church leaders because their approaches to ministry are so effective. These flagship church resources reveal the proven ideas, programs, and principles that these churches have put into practice.

Flagship Church Resources currently available:

- *Doing Life With God*
- *Doing Life With God 2*
- *The Visual Edge:*
  Compelling Video Connectors for Your Worship Experience
- *Mission-Driven Worship:*
  Helping Your Changing Church Celebrate God
- *An Unstoppable Force:*
  Daring to Become the Church God Had in Mind
- *A Follower's Life:*
  12 Group Studies on What It Means to Walk With Jesus
- *Leadership Essentials for Children's Ministry*
- *Keeping Your Head Above Water:*
  Refreshing Insights for Church Leadership
- *Seeing Beyond Church Walls:*
  Action Plans for Touching Your Community
- *unLearning Church:*
  Just When You Thought You Had Leadership All Figured Out!

With more to follow!

empowering teenagers through God's grace

the winning
spirit

Chris Hill

Flagship church resources
from Group Publishing

Group's R.E.A.L. Guarantee to you:

Every Group resource incorporates our R.E.A.L. approach to ministry—a unique philosophy that results in long-term retention and life transformation. It's ministry that's:

This is EARL. He's R.E.A.L. mixed up. (Get it?)

Relational
Because student-to-student interaction enhances learning and builds Christian friendships.

Experiential
Because what students experience sticks with them up to 9 times longer than what they simply hear or read.

Applicable
Because the aim of Christian education is to be both hearers and doers of the Word.

Learner-based
Because students learn more and retain it longer when the process is designed according to how they learn best.

The Winning Spirit
Empowering Teenagers Through God's Grace
Copyright © 2002 Chris Hill

Visit our Web site: **www.grouppublishing.com**

Credits
Editor: Amy Simpson
Creative Development Editor: Dave Thornton
Chief Creative Officer: Joani Schultz
Copy Editor: Lyndsay E. Gerwing
Art Director: Nancy Serbus
Cover Art Director: Jeff A. Storm
Cover Designer: Blukazoo Studio
Cover Photographer: Daniel Treat
Computer Graphic Artist: Joyce Douglas
Production Manager: Dodie Tipton

Library of Congress Cataloging-in-Publication Data
Hill, E. Christopher, 1968-
　　　The winning spirit : empowering teenagers through God's grace / by
Chris Hill.
　　　　　p.　　cm.
Includes bibliographical references.
　　ISBN 0-7644-2396-7 (pbk. : alk. paper)
　　1. Church work with youth.　I. Title.
BV4447 .H495 2002
259' .23--dc21　　　　　　　　　　　　　　　　　　　　　　2002002597

10 9 8 7 6 5 4 3 2 1　　　11 10 09 08 07 06 05 04 03 02

Printed in the United States of America.

"Young people will identify with *The Winning Spirit*. Author Chris Hill encourages all ages and proves that anyone can be a winner with proper coaching."

Troyvoi Hicks, Principal, Aspire Public Schools

"I highly recommend this book to every pastor, youth minister, teacher, and parent. In *The Winning Spirit*, Chris Hill shares how we can help influence and empower teenagers to be winners."

Craig W. Hagin, Youth Minister, RHEMA Bible Church

"Pastor Chris Hill has been a tremendously valuable influence for our youth ministry. His wisdom and vision exemplify that he is in fact a winner, and I believe that many will benefit from his thoughts."

Bishop T.D. Jakes Sr., Senior Pastor, The Potter's House of Dallas, Inc.

"From the first few pages of *The Winning Spirit*, I knew Chris Hill had hit the mark. Too many young people are hurt by assuming they are or will become losers in life. This book is a shot of adrenaline to the minds and hearts of our youth and raises hopes that, I believe, for years to come will be felt."

Dave Burrows, Pastor, Youth Alive Ministries & Bahamas Faith Ministries

"Chris has hit a homerun! This is exactly what youth pastors, leaders, and volunteers need to know about teens today. This book is a must for all who are serious about the teen ministry they serve."

Chris Binion, Youth Pastor, Xtremedge, Newport News, Virginia

"Each time Chris Hill ministers he projects a 'winning spirit' that is a reflection of his inner man. Each year his winning spirit infects thousands of our teens to a fresh commitment in Jesus Christ."

Tom Madden, Youth Ministries Coordinator,
Church of God International Department of Youth & Christian Education

---

This book is dedicated to the five J's in my life: Jesus, my Savior;
Juanita, my mother; Joy, my lover; Junior, my successor; and Jakes,
my mentor—I soar on your prayers, dance in your sunshine,
and stand on your wisdom.

---

acknowledgments

To all the twenty-first-century Samuels who are still looking for David—pour it on!

To my Potter's House church family, pastors, elders and ministers, and youth— thanks for all your support.

To all of my dear family, ministry partners, and faithful friends—you teach me.

To Amy and all the folks at Group Publishing—you make me look marvelous! For this I am in your debt.

To Rev. Dr. Craig McMullen—thanks for believing in me before I could see me.

contents

introduction

a secret

A secret lingers in the hearts of America's teenagers. This secret is so dear to them and yet so destructive that, left unchecked, it threatens to sabotage their faith, their families, and their futures. This secret, like some poisonous gas, threatens to float unseen into their lives and choke off all their potential, all their power, and all their dreams. It is a silent predator in the jungle of their destiny, lurking deftly through the underbrush of their psyche, threatening to devour their potential alive and whole before they have made their mark on the future.

This secret must be discovered. It must be defined, dealt with, and dispelled before more precious teenagers fall under its influence and power.

This secret is whispered aloud only when no one is looking. It is tearfully breathed into wet pillows between desperate sobs. It has risen like a curse from the dogmatic lips of unkind hearts—hearts so darkened with malice that the light of Christ has never shined upon them. This secret has been spoken by twisted mouths, which through clenched teeth have spoken words of disgust and hatred. This secret has been hurled like a stone at young people, even from the mouths of parents, counselors, and teachers—people who should love them too deeply to cut them so cruelly.

This secret has been inscribed on the walls of their hearts by unfair circumstances and then cemented to their self-esteem by rejections and abuse. Pain and loss have reinforced this thinking, and like a symphony of pain, this secret has been repeated through the movements of their lives. It has been repeated at the schoolhouse; in the images of the media; through their songs, videos, and movies.

The secret has been told and retold so many times, sometimes with words and sometimes with pictures. The meaning has been repeated so often that it now rolls around their minds like a ball bearing set loose in a car engine. Though the engine still runs, it echoes with the sound of something that is loose. And so their thoughts echo with the sound of this dark secret. Their minds are still running, but with a foreign object constantly messing up the works.

This secret must not be allowed to loiter any longer in the shadows; the bright light of Christ's truth must shine on it.

This secret must be shared. We must shout it from the rooftops and then shatter it by casting it down from that great height. It must be robbed of its power and unmasked as a lie.

The secret is very simple, but its strength to conquer our youth is locked up in its simplicity. **Too many of America's teenagers secretly believe they are losers.**

born to lose

They believe they have been born to lose in the game of life; they believe they cannot win. They secretly believe they are losers, despite the odds in their favor, the support of their families, and the communities of faith in which they have been raised.

Even if they live in the best and most expensive communities, they are not convinced of their personal victories. Even young people who have been handed the best in life will hide their lights within the purple haze of heroin and designer drugs or drown their dreams in kegs filled with potent imported lagers. They are rich in substance but poor in perception, and they believe they are losers.

Nor are other young people convinced of their personal victories by virtue of their ability to survive the vilest of living conditions, in the most poor and dangerous communities. Even those who used to see themselves as the greatest of survivors no longer view themselves in this optimistic light. In times past, they prided themselves on their ability to live nobly in poverty, to take life's lemons and make lemonade, and to see the positive strength one requires to live in a negative environment. They no longer see themselves as winners, and there is little pride in the teenagers who survive these impoverished communities. Many of these teenagers believe themselves to be losers.

So both in the ghettos of America and in her garden communities, our teenagers really think they are losers. So they live out losing scenarios and make losing choices and take losing chances with their lives and destinies based in and on their silent, secret belief that they cannot win. They lack the firm Christ-centered conviction that is supposed to teach them they cannot lose, so they believe they cannot win. In the rich neighborhoods and in the rural towns, they look at themselves in both full-length mirrors suspended over marble vanities and simple mirrors that serve as doors to medicine cabinets. They say in one accord from both sides of the track, "I am a loser!"

Publicly they smile and laugh loudly—sometimes too loudly. And they sing and dance with gaiety; they are simply painting a shallow whitewash over the uneven walls of painful perception that surround them. Sometimes even though they line the padded pews of our sanctuaries and sing out our hymns and liturgies without a pause or a second thought, they secretly believe they are losers, and only their losing decisions tell on them. In reality when these teens look at themselves in the mirror, instead of being heartened with the endless number of possibilities that confront them in the realm of the future, they are overwhelmed by the dark shadows of defeat that have chased them from their past into their present. These teenagers look resolutely in the mirror and shape their fingers into an L, left forefinger straight up and the thumb fully extended to the right, and say with lips that make no sound, "I am such a loser!"

behind the secret

Maybe their families, their schools, or their communities have reinforced this secret so profoundly into their thinking. Maybe their backgrounds have contained so much rejection or they have been physically, mentally, or sexually abused. Maybe their hopes have been shipwrecked by their parents' divorce (either legal or emotional) or train-wrecked by some other personal tragedy—loss of a loved one or a schoolmate or even a national landmark. Maybe they have watched too much death and destruction on television. Even the news stations have fallen desperately in love with repeating images of tragedy, turmoil, and terror until they are permanently and indelibly imprinted on our long-term memories and both young and old have seen the shadow of death and terror. Maybe they have experienced so much disappointment that they have grown disillusioned with life, adults, or God's Word.

Whatever the reasons, they now believe they are powerless to overcome this life. They believe firmly that whatever actions they take, the outcome of their lives will be negative and painful. They fight with depression and substance abuse, violence and suicide, apathy and hopelessness, because they believe that even when they are winning big, they are being set up to lose bigger. This secret is killing them, and in them the very future of our churches, our families, our communities, and our nation is dying.

confronting the secret

It is high time that Christians begin to confront this secret head-on. No longer skirting or shirking our responsibility, but armed with the power of the grace of God, we must begin to batter away at this spiritual stronghold in the lives of our teenagers. Whether we are parents or pastors, teachers or preachers, counselors or coaches, we have to begin to empower these teenagers with a winning spirit.

We must begin to teach our teenagers that God's grace has already won their race. Their future has been fixed and assured by Christ's finished work on Calvary. When Christ won on the cross, he assured that his victory would affect and infect us who have hidden our lives inside him. He made us all more than conquerors in Christ Jesus. But if we are to dispel the dark cloud of this secret, we who are Christians must take this thing further. We must begin to live our lives as both role models and whole models. We must demonstrate and represent the power of God's grace to those who are standing against great odds and living in the midst of terrible situations. We must help them to say, "I am a winner because the 'winning one' is inside me."

In this book we will explore together, through God's Word, how we who are called to teach and influence teenagers can empower them through the amazing grace of God. We will explain and outline through both precept and example how to—through faith in Christ—take, inundate, and then saturate teenagers who believe they are losers with the winning spirit.

Chris Hill
January 16, 2002
Dallas, Texas

prologue

redena's story

It was a Thursday afternoon. Redena walked into my small youth office in the inner city of Boston, Massachusetts. Redena was a beautiful, brown-faced, bright-eyed girl of fifteen. She was usually lighted up with a smile and quick to laugh—a typical middle child, easy to please and aiming to please. But when she came into my little office and sat down on that old couch, she had a distraught look on her face. I could tell she was thinking deeply about something because she always brought such a light with her, the kind of light that children who are born in adversity seem to carry inside. That day the light was not on. She sat quietly in the corner, so I began to ask her what was on her heart.

Redena never knew her father. While she did have older brothers and sisters, they were all products of her mother's relationships with different men other than her father. Her mother came to know Christ later on in life, but even in finding Christ, her mother had not been completely healed from the pains of her past. Salvation had not made Redena's mother a better communicator, nor had it given her a strong, connected relationship with her daughter. So even though her mother was "there," Redena was still desperately lonely.

Simply because people come to Christ doesn't mean they have the ability to raise children correctly or to communicate effectively within their families. There's a difference between finding Christ and finding life in Christ: When you have only found Christ, you're ready to go to heaven; but when you have found life in Christ, you're ready to live on earth with the earnest expectation of also going to heaven.

And so Redena walked into my youth office and placed me in a strange position—a fatherly position in the sense that I had become one of the only positive men in her life. She was not much younger then I was at the time, and I could not reasonably have been her father, but through the power of the gospel, I had become her father. And by virtue of a constant commitment, I had earned the right to speak as a spiritual father in her life.

I asked her what the sad face was all about, and she told me quite resolutely that she had decided to have a baby.

my reaction

Now remember that Redena was only fifteen years old. She herself was still a baby and was not even sexually active at that time, but she was beginning to contemplate becoming sexually active in order to have a baby. This was not so much because she wanted a sexual relationship; she just wanted the result—a child.

A child to love her completely and unconditionally.

By this time I had lived in the inner city long enough to know where this thinking was coming from. In order to understand the heart desires of some of America's most hurting kids, you have to get up underneath the family systems. Otherwise, you will view the thought processes of our children as deranged and deviant, and you will misjudge the children, who are only thinking in a way that is consistent with how they have been trained.

Because Redena's father had abandoned the family, her mother now had to work two or three jobs—cleaning jobs, hard jobs—in order to support the family. In her heart, Redena's mother had a real desire to initiate positive conversation and to reinforce biblical principles in the life of her daughter. But the unfortunate, unfair, and overwhelming demands of just keeping the lights on and the heat on and a roof over their heads ate into the positive time and energy that Redena's mother had to give.

It is easy to recline in the easy chair of our "Ozzie and Harriet" family system and give pointless lectures to urban parents about quality and quantity time. But the harsh reality of the struggle to keep things afloat has to factor into a realistic teaching model for our modern parents. Church leaders have to wake up and smell the coffee or else our tirades on family values will be met with as much disdain in the church house as they are now met with in the public square.

So here was Redena's mother, having to take care of the financial needs of an entire family. And here was Redena, crying out for someone who would love her unconditionally and exclusively. Redena wrestled with the question "Where do I find that type of love?" Her fifteen-year-old mind answered with a baby.

my advice

"A baby!" After I regained my cool and began to look behind the request and see the real need, I began to address her thinking. I began to scold her lovingly, as only her pastor can, and to force her to consider the reasoning that led to her conclusion to get pregnant. "The reason you want to have this baby," I said, "is that you want someone who will love you exclusively without distraction and without being busy, without being drawn away. Wanting to love a child and wanting a child to love you is not a negative thing. But the result of you having a child would be the child living the exact same life that you're living right now."

Her eyes opened wider, so I kept on talking. "She would grow up longing for a father's attention, just like you. She would grow up longing for proper financial support, just like you. She would want the type of life that is enjoyable and has recreation and downtime and some level of ease."

Redena nodded; she was listening now. A quick tear rolled down her brown cheek.

I said, "Baby-girl" (I call almost all the girls in my youth church by that title), "the problem is that if you go out there and have a baby, you would create a child that loves you but feels the same way about life that you do. So while I understand the feelings you have, and in some ways your feelings are justified, if you run out there and get pregnant, you will just cause that pain to be handed down to the next generation. Baby-girl, you decide to break this cycle of pain, or you will find yourself making your child go through the same hell that you're going through right now."

That Thursday afternoon I gave Redena a piece of advice that I have given ever since to young girls who are wrestling with this "love" issue. I told her to go down to the mall and to buy the smallest and cutest puppy in the pet store. I told her that the dog wouldn't fix everything wrong in her life but that the purchase of that small dog would fulfill a small part of that need she was dealing with. The puppy would come without all of the negative attachments that come with having a child before one is ready to raise a child, while still out of the confines of a biblical, balanced, and financially sound marital structure. Life decisions are like dogs—they always come with fleas. The trick is to have enough emotional pesticide available to deal with those fleas.

Redena took my advice and went on to finish school and is now married. They still don't have a baby, but they do have the dog.

chapter 1

winners and losers

"As water reflects a face, so a man's heart reflects the man" (Proverbs 27:19).

I opened this book with the story of Redena because it typifies what my course in youth ministry has been over the last nineteen years. I have learned that losers have children and they teach their children how to lose. In fact, after a number of years, any honest minister—or any honest person for that matter—can quickly identify and categorize people into two different and distinct categories: winners and losers.

Most people are too nice or too politically correct to "break it down" so directly or succinctly, even though it is how we think about people. But I dare you to take the time to truly listen to people, teenagers quite specifically. In doing so you will quickly realize that on some semiconscious level, all of us are constantly grouping people under those two different headings.

Polite society doesn't allow us to voice our opinions. But just let me take you to any high school cafeteria in America, and I can quickly show you where the winners sit. Upon closer inspection we would also discover the eating place for the losers.

We all knew the winners and the losers.

We all know who the winners and losers are; we adults are just too polite to say so. But the teenagers who are caught in the cycle of losing know who they are and are in desperate need of our help.

I remember when I was a skinny teenager growing up in Boston. We would often organize and play pickup games of basketball throughout the summer on the paved side streets that didn't get very much car traffic. Two strong captains, both always unquestionably winners, would buck up with confident fingers pointing at each other and then begin to pick teammates. This painful process of selection would quickly identify the winners, who would be selected quickly and with great joy, and the losers, who were always the last to be selected— and even when selected might be chosen with annoyance and anger, depending on the grace and confidence of the captain. At times one or two losers would be left standing there on the pavement, unwanted. **We all knew the winners and the losers.**

Even those of us who would consider ourselves to be good Christians, if cornered into a position of unusual and uncharacteristic honesty, can walk through the membership roles of our churches and tell you who are the winners and who are the losers.

they're everywhere

Now if you are thinking that I am talking about color or class or socioeconomic or educational level, you are far from the point, because I could show you losers who live in the best of neighborhoods and drive the newest automobiles and have a virtual alphabet of degrees behind their names. But in many cases, if you scratch underneath their gold-plated exteriors, you will find losers who cannot maintain marriages, maintain households, control their careers, or raise positive children.

Justice would have left us standing in the sidelines of life, but grace selected us and, grace pulls us into the game.

Conversely, I could take you into housing developments and trailer parks that have more rats than children and where children play with roaches like household pets, and in the midst of abject poverty and absolute squalor, I can show you winners who are successfully navigating the stormy seas of life without allowing the waves of adversity to swamp their skiffs of destiny. I could show you single parents raising children to be champions, despite their environments. I could show you parents using nurture to overcome the curses of nature.

I could show you children who call on the power of Christ to overcome the destructive power of the streets. I could show you winners who are being empowered, neither through a governmental system nor through an outreach of the church, but by an invisible hand that is pulling them up by their bootstraps—the gracious grip of our God.

So winning speaks not to some objective level of accomplishment that would only be fair or truly relevant if everyone is allowed to begin on some level playing field. No, winning is the subjective level of personal achievement that can only be ascertained by spiritual contemplation and introspection.

captain jesus

The good news of the gospel is that Captain Jesus still selected us for his team, even though we were all destined to be losers. Justice would have left us standing on the sidelines of life, but grace selected us, and grace pulls us into the game. This game of life, Jesus has already "fixed" so that in the end we can only and always win the game.

Every person has a God-given task to accomplish. Every person has a personal mission that echoes in the spirit. The winner is that person who can answer the nagging voice of unconscious potential which calls him or her to a private and personal level of excellence. The winner hears that voice and says with all confidence and boldness, "I am heading in the direction of my destiny. I am striving toward my God-given goals." The winner is the one who not only learns to endure the day-to-day striving but, through the mysterious power of God's grace, also has learned to love the race. This is the winning spirit.

I believe that every parent, minister, teacher, counselor, and youth worker should know how to take teenagers who are caught in losing systems and then teach those young people, regardless of their backgrounds or situations, how to win. We should be able to impart something to them that goes beyond their heads and into their hearts: an attitude, an outlook, and a spirit—a winning spirit.

———————————————————————— youth ministry insights

Thinking about your youth ministry program, consider the answers to these questions:

- How many of your students would society consider to be losers?

- How many of your students would society consider to be winners?

- How many of your students perceive themselves as losers?

- What programs or plans can you use to change that perception?

- What are some loser-to-winner success stories you're aware of, either inside or outside your youth ministry? What factors were behind these success stories?

- How can your youth ministry program help turn losers into winners?

anatomy of a winner

"I praise you because I am fearfully and wonderfully made; your works are wonderful, I know that full well" (Psalm 139:14).

Winners are not people who never lose, for winners can lose but are never lost. They never lose their hope or their spirit or their mission in life. Though cast down, they cannot be destroyed (2 Corinthians 4:8-9). Winners can have all the odds set against them and their backs against the wall and still snatch a victory out of the mouth of defeat. Winners are not people who have never tasted the agony of defeat, but winners are people who have brushed off the dust of depression and picked themselves up off the side of the road and found a way to win in the game of life.

To a winner a loss is just research. To a loser a loss is just another rehearsal.

Winners always win. Even when they lose, they are just gathering more information about themselves and the challenges they are facing so they can learn more about how to win. **To a winner a loss is just research. To a loser a loss is just another rehearsal.**

born out of a win

The moment of truth for winners—the moment when we begin to teach them that they were born to win—is when they truly realize that their lives were born through a winning situation. Despite the circumstances that surrounded or even produced their lives, the fact that they are alive and that they survived the strange and mysterious process that produces a human life is in and of itself a win.

"O Lord, our Lord, how majestic is your name in all the earth! You have set your glory above the heavens. From the lips of children and infants you have ordained praise" (Psalm 8:1-2a).

There were millions and millions of your father's sperm that raced toward your mother's egg, an egg that God had positioned at just the right time to receive them. Out of the millions of sperm that raced toward that finish line of life, just one made it to the egg. It won.

Then the miracle of conception began; and your cells began to grow and replicate; and from one strange form to another strange form, a human being emerged. Hidden in your mother's womb, the creative workshop of the Creator, you emerged first from the form of an egg to the form of a lizard to the form of a mammal and then to the form of a human. This is one of the miracles of childbirth. God walks us through all the forms of the lesser creatures, like a composer walks us through the movements of a classical symphony, only to crescendo our creation by forming us into humans. The human fetus looks like the other created animals when it is in the process of development, but at the end of the process, it becomes a person. Just to be a person is a win.

It is as if God is playing some kind of practical joke on those who put their faith in the musings of Charles Darwin. God shows us that what so many evolutionists believe took millions of years to evolve on the earth, he produces in a matter of months. In the workshop of the womb, he knits together a human. The evolutionist can see that to God a day is as a thousand years.

Just to be a person is a win.

During this precarious process of gestation, the nine months that were required to produce your life, a myriad of things could have happened to you. You were defenseless in your mother's womb, and any number of sicknesses could have overwhelmed you. Poor nutrition could have snuffed out the flickering candle of your life. High blood pressure or low heart rate could have gripped you. Your mother could have fallen into some physical tragedy that also could have crushed your little life. The hand of the abortionist could have reached into your sanctuary of the womb and ended the reproductive process. All these things could have happened to you. They have happened to babies all over the world, every day, every hour, and every minute since humanity has walked the surface of this green globe. And yet none of these things happened to you. You won, even before you got here!

the crowning moment

Then you were born. Doctors and nurses use a special term to describe the moment when a baby presents its head during the birth process. They call it *crowning*. I think this term is so appropriate because even though they're speaking technically about the positioning of the baby, I cannot help but think that the doctors and nurses are speaking a spiritual truth they may not even be aware of.

As your mother, with the help of God, pushed you out of her womb, you were crowned a winner. You had finished the process, and like a marathoner you rounded the last corner, leaned into the finish line, and were crowned the winner (Psalm 8:5).

The principle is simple. When you emerged alive from the womb, you had just won that first race. Of all the things that could have happened to you in the womb while you were still in that defenseless state, God's grace spared you, and you won that first contest to live. You crossed the finish line and instantly began another race: the human race.

Henri was a bright-eyed, round-headed boy in our youth church. He was short and squat, but even when he was a preteen, you could see the muscles starting to knit together into round, strong knots underneath his dark chocolate-brown skin. He had the makings of a good football running back—low center of gravity and strong as an ox. But unlike most of the jocks I have encountered in my youth churches over the years, Henri was also very, very smart—book smart.

This sparked my attention because like most of his peers, Henri was a fatherless boy who lived in one of the toughest housing developments in the city, but despite his environment he seemed to be such a happy and well-adjusted boy. His example of a winning spirit is what compelled me to study his family system to see what his mother was doing to raise such a "good" kid in such a bad place.

I sat one afternoon with his mother to find out what she was "feeding" the boy, and what she told me has blessed my life from that day to this one. She told me that a man had raped her one tragic night, and from that hideous act of hatred had come Henri. When she discovered she was pregnant with the seed of this monster, Henri's mother made a critical decision. She decided that she would not concentrate on the part of her child that was made by the rapist but that she would concentrate on raising the part of her child that was her own.

She celebrated his life as a wonderful gift of God. She embraced his coming like a flower soaks in a spring rain. She decided not to abort the baby but to bring him to term and then to raise him with all the love, support, and nurture that she could muster. She went with him to football games, and she taught him how to throw. She went to all his school programs and got to know his teachers.

She decided to improve herself, to become the best role model of excellence that she could be for her child. She finished her degrees while in the projects, lying on the floor next to him at night, writing her own papers while she helped him with his homework. She decided that with the grace of God, she would raise a wonderful man who would be an excellent son, father, and husband. She decided that even though he was conceived in violence, Henri would not be raised in violence. She decided that Henri would be raised in love, support, and the belly of the church.

I have never in my life seen a mother more filled with the winning spirit than was Henri's mother, and she was rewarded for her sacrifice. Henri graduated from high school, college, and then medical school. He is a successful doctor today and is happily married. But if you ask him how he feels about his mother, this heavily muscled mound of a man will melt into tears.

throw yourself a party

Because people can't remember the day they were born, we rely on our parents and loved ones to rehearse for us the first days of our lives on this earth. Like the beginning of a cassette tape, the beginnings of our memories seem not to have the material to record those first events. I believe that because we don't remember the event of birth, we easily overlook that triumph—the triumph of life and the emergence from the womb.

But in shaping a winner, we must always consider and celebrate the gift of life. This is why I believe that the celebration of a birthday, through dinners or parties or some kind of special event, is so important. We need to have a celebration to commemorate a contest that was won, even though most of us cannot remember it. Put your party hat on and invite your friends, because even though you cannot remember that you won that first contest, the fact that you are here is enough evidence to prove that you won.

Even if you don't have anyone to invite or if there is no one to share that moment of celebration with, light a candle and bake a three-dollar cake because on the day you were born, God gave you the best and greatest gift of all. It is called life, and every day that we live, we unwrap that gift to discover the contents of his gift of grace.

I have spent endless hours with teenagers and their parents, getting them to recapture the wonder and miracle of that first day of life. If we could remember and somehow bottle the overwhelming feeling of victory and triumph from that first day of life, then in a time of darkness, depression, and despair, we could drink deeply from this bottle of thankful remembrance. We could stay drunk with that spirit, the winning spirit. And we would not need alcohol or any other substance to drown our sorrows.

——————————————————————— youth ministry **insights

Consider the answers to these questions. It would be helpful to discuss your answers with your spouse, a ministry partner, or a close friend.

* What are some events in your life that you didn't realize were victories?

* How did God's grace work through those events in your life?

* How have your past victories prepared you for what might lie ahead along your life's path?

* How can you celebrate the victories God's grace has brought about in your life?

winners always win

"Then Samson prayed to the Lord, 'O Sovereign Lord, remember me. O God, please strengthen me just once more, and let me with one blow get revenge on the Philistines for my two eyes.' Then Samson reached toward the two central pillars on which the temple stood. Bracing himself against them, his right hand on the one and his left hand on the other, Samson said, 'Let me die with the Philistines!' Then he pushed with all his might, and down came the temple on the rulers and all the people in it. Thus he killed many more when he died than while he lived" (Judges 16:28-30).

Winners see the world differently from other people. They seem to see the world through rose-colored glasses and champagne showers, with an optimistic spin. For winners the glass is not half empty; it is half full and much more than they needed to drink anyway. Winners, those who are so filled with this winning spirit, are undeterred by what is lacking in their lives because they are so focused on their goals and are constantly and consistently encouraged by what they already have in their lives that will help them to achieve and make real their dreams.

In working with teenagers who are caught in losing systems, the positive adults in their lives—whether we are parents, Christian youth workers, or counselors—have to teach those teenagers how to perceive life as winners do. Winners always expect life to deal them a winning hand and are always prepared to win, regardless of the cards they are dealt. Winners expect to win, and often because they expect to win, they do.

To some, this attitude of expectation seems to be a setup for a great letdown. Some people believe it is dangerous to teach teenagers to expect the best out of life. They believe we should put some disclaimer into our messages of hope, an out-clause lest our young people begin to dream too high or hope too much. These doomsayers, who masquerade under the guise of common sense and propriety, would have us believe that the grace of God is limited by the circumstances that hinder people. But God's grace knows no limitation.

expecting to win

As with the three Hebrew boys Shadrach, Meshach, and Abednego (Daniel 3), God's grace always comes not with a disclaimer but with a "proclaimer." Shadrach, Meshach, and Abednego proclaimed to their Babylonian masters that they would not bow to their masters' strange gods and that they were expecting their God to save them from the flames of the furnace. But they also proclaimed that even if God did not save them, they still would not bow and that they were willing to die standing rather than to live bowing. To the Hebrew boys, burning was not a loss, but bowing was. This is true with the winner as well. Getting burned by a defeat is not a loss to a winner. But bowing to fear and falling to the pressure to back away from convictions is a crushing defeat.

You must understand that this expecting-to-win attitude, coupled with the proclamation that they would not bend, buckle, or bow under the weight of persecution or tribulation, is the winning spirit that witnessed loudest to the Babylonian king. Courage is not just entering a battle expecting to win; it is the willingness to enter the battle in the first place. Winners decide to exercise courage and enter the arena of conflict but have a worldview that does not allow them to sit in the arena and contemplate how outnumbered they are and how heavily the odds are stacked against them. Winners embrace the struggle and, in their heart of hearts, believe that they will win. Even if they don't win the particular struggle, they will see themselves as winners for simply having the courage to walk into the arena against such odds.

I do not believe that David expected to lose in his classic struggle against Goliath, but I believe that even if he had lost, David would have demonstrated more courage than every other man in the armies of King Saul. And that small victory—to have more courage than a king and all his trained and bloodied soldiers—in and of itself would have been a win.

This principle is real on every athletic field on the surface of the earth. No coach teaches his or her athletes to enter into a serious athletic contest expecting to lose the match. The principle is real in the marketplace, for no successful salesperson enters serious sales negotiations expecting not to close the deal. And this same principle is also real on the home front, for no successful marriage relationship was built by two people who married with the expectation of the marriage ending in a painful divorce.

Thank God that his grace is able to help us when we fail, but his grace is also available to help us succeed. Too often teenagers who are living in losing family systems, caught in losing habits, or raised in losing socioeconomic systems are spoonfed a diet of disclaimers instead of challenged to change their lives. It is the job of the positive adult to influence the lives of teenagers and to so infuse youth with a winning spirit that teenagers begin to think like winners.

you pass what you catch

Parents and youth workers have to have a winning spirit in order to pass that spirit on to young people. As a child in kindergarten, I used to play a game called Wonder Ball. We would pass the ball around and around the circle until the music stopped. Like the Wonder Ball, you cannot pass the spirit of an overcomer around the circle of your home or your youth ministry until you yourself have caught the wonder of your life and calling.

So often the negative experiences and losing attitudes that we adults have accumulated over the years get passed down to the teenagers who come in contact with our lives. We got divorced, so we teach our children to enter marriage relationships with their hearts prepared to experience divorce and separation. We never achieved our dreams, so we teach our children to have easily attainable goals, and we drain their spirits of all lofty dreams and aspirations. We have low self-esteem or a poor world outlook, and like a contagious virus we pass that soul sickness on to our children through the breast milk of our counsel.

I have met many parents and youth workers who meant no harm by passing on their negativity; in fact, they meant to protect their young people from harsh disappointments and from broken dreams. But in doing so, they actually robbed their charges of the opportunity of experiencing wonder and greatness in their lives. And they actually set in motion some self-fulfilling prophecies that their children began to live out because they were built to lose and not built to win. These adults passed on a losing spirit, not because they really wanted to but because it was all they had to pass on.

Adults who want to teach teenagers how to become winners must first examine themselves to see what kind of worldview they have and how their limitations and expectations color their counsel, preaching, or parenting.

Henry Ford said it well: "Whether you believe you can do a thing or not, you are right." We have to teach our young people to think they can. And if we think our children can, they will think so too. Even failing, they will discover the depths of the grace of God, which can help them win in any situation and help them survive a loss until they turn it into a win.

winners always win

"The mighty Samson has fallen." The word must have spread like wildfire all over Israel. Certainly the Philistine lords must have called a holiday or a feast day of some sort to celebrate how they had finally captured the judge and champion of Israel who had caused them so much pain and embarrassment. Samson, who had single-handedly decimated whole armies. Samson, who had stood as an army of one against the Philistine hoard. Samson had fallen.

Samson had fallen not to a sword or an arrow. Nor under the hand of a mightier man, for there was no one mightier than this man. No, Samson had fallen to a woman. Delilah had found out the secret of his strength. She had pried out of his heart a secret that no man was strong enough to pry out of his hand. Delilah had bested him not on the field of battle but in the battlefield of his heart. She had found out the riddle of his strength and then sold him to the lords of the Philistines. Samson had fallen in love, and then he had fallen in battle.

This was juicy stuff, worthy to be emblazed on the covers of our modern tabloids. Can you imagine how the people of that age must have received these tasty morsels of gossip and shared them in graphic detail with their friends and neighbors until the word covered the land like ash after a volcanic eruption?

The mighty Samson had fallen. They had shaved him, beaten him, and chained him up like an animal. See how he had fallen. They had plucked out his eyes, and a little child led he who had been the leader of a nation. The hero now had a handicap, and the lords of the Philistines were celebrating his sufferings.

But they could not count Samson out, because he knew too much about winning. He had experienced too many victories in his life. He had walked with God too much to be discounted like some rookie. He was a seasoned soldier who had seen bloody battle before. God's grace had snatched a victory out of the jaws of defeat so many times in the course of Samson's life that, even blind and led about like an animal, Samson was still not bereft of hope. Even with his head shaved and his honor gone. Even though everyone was laughing at him and the whole region knew how and what Delilah had done to him. Samson had not forgotten about God's grace. Samson called out to the Lord for just enough strength to win again. He asked God for just enough grace to end the story right. Grace not to change the past or even to escape the Philistines and secure his future; Samson asked for enough grace to show his captors that God can take a loss and turn it into a win.

Most people would have told Samson to be happy with his lot. To be satisfied that he was still alive. But Samson was so much a winner that he expected a win to once again come out of a loss. He was looking for something sweet to again come out of the carcass of defeat (Judges 14:8-9).

And so blind Samson placed his hands against the wall and cried out to the God of all grace for enough strength to bring down the house of his captors. And the God of all grace heard him and granted his request. And in death Samson killed more of his enemies than he had ever killed in life. He was a winner. He was a winner not because he had never lost a battle, for without question he lost the battle of the heart to Delilah. Samson was a winner because the defeat beat him up but never beat him down. Even when he was beat up, caught up in a cycle of losing, he was biding his time and crying out to God for one chance, one opportunity to win. And when that opportunity presented itself, he seized it without fear.

learning from a loss

To a winner a loss is just research. A loss simply serves as a teaching tool to a winner—a tool that teaches him or her how to be successful next time. Samson's crippling loss just taught him that he had to remain God-conscious and God-centered, because his strength was not in himself but was totally dependent upon the grace and favor of God. It was God's grace that was and had been empowering him, and if he were to win this last and most important battle, he would have to get back into God's good graces.

Samson learned the lesson and cried out to God, and God empowered him to bring the roof down on his enemies. Obviously Samson learned from his loss. And if we can teach young people how to learn from their losses, then we can teach them how to win.

Just as a boxer's trainer sits down with the boxer and studies videotapes with the fighter, youth workers must sit down with teenagers and examine the losing cycle that is trying to hold on to them. Replay the videotapes of their lives, and show them where their opponents have been jabbing through their defenses. Sometimes the cycle has been running through their neighborhoods or family systems for so long that we have to run the life-tapes of others who are caught in the cycle and then show teenagers how to stop the attack from getting to their heads and knocking them down or out.

With Redena, I was able to show how she was just reacting to the cycle of father-lessness into which she had been born and to play back the life-tape of her own family to help show her why she had to avoid premarital sexual activity and teenage pregnancy. Until someone had the patience to sit down and carefully show her the cycle of losing thinking she was caught in, Redena was heading toward making decisions that would have held her in the cycle. This is why positive parents, counselors, ministers, and youth workers are so very necessary. These positive adults can be the trainers and coaches that teach teenagers how to see the cycles and can help shape and reshape how they see life so that they can learn how to win.

Susan was born with lupus. Her long hair fell past her shoulders and framed her angular face. She was thin like a model and stood on two legs that seemed almost too thin to hold her lanky frame. Her eyes were yellowed and jaundiced, but her smile was active and powerful, filled with life and hope. Susan's mother was dead before I met her, from the same debilitating disease. Because of her mother's death, her grandparents were raising Susan, and they doted over her like a mother hen over her chicks.

But I never treated her any differently than any of the other young ladies in the youth church, and I didn't allow the other youth workers to single her out for special treatment or special consideration. I nicknamed her (as I do with most people) and recommended her for jobs at the church, pushed her, and challenged her to live out each day with grace and gusto. I told her that she was a heroine in the comic book of her own life, and it was up to her to make sure that she had a happy ending. I tried to exemplify an attitude of a winner around her, a winning spirit that looks up even though the situation often looks grim.

I began to see Susan change. She stopped whining and started winning. She stopped being a spoiled little girl whose grandparents, understandably, wanted to shield her from the hardships of life. She started to take responsibility for her own happiness, achievement, and overall enjoyment.

She was dying, but she was more alive than many of the thousands of youth I have preached to over these years. She was always on the go, always shopping or cooking or going to the beauty shop. She was alive and thoroughly determined to eat each day of life whole, sucking the juice out of every moment God had given her.

She knew she was sick. The numerous trips to the hospital for medicines, examinations, and blood transfusions would force anyone to deal with mortality. She was not in denial, nor was she deluded from the reality of her own death. In fact she thought the rest of us, who were healthy, were the ones in denial because she had accepted that she could die any day now—and most of us haven't realized that we, too, could die any day because tomorrow is not promised to anyone.

She was in a losing situation, but she refused to lose. She finished high school and went to college. She sang in the choir at our youth church and went on all the trips. She had boyfriends, she argued with her sometimes-overprotective grandparents, and for all intents and purposes lived a normal and happy life. She lived one day at a time, with the grace of God empowering her each day.

And she still lives, each day by God's grace. Susan has defied the doctor's diagnosis and has defied all the odds against her and is still living with lupus. And I mean living! She is alive and winning to this hour because she has learned how to win, even when life seems to deal a losing hand. **Because whiners never win and winners never whine.**

Whiners never win and winners never whine.

live to win

Susan now lives to win. She understands that every day for her, as it is for all of us, is a win. Just to live is to win. Every day that you open your eyes and you are lying on a bed and not in a casket, that is a winning day.

Every day that you walk on the ground and don't have six feet of dirt over your head, that is a win. It's a privilege just to have life and breath and thought and dreams. These small intangible things cannot be purchased with all the money in the world, and yet these are some of the most valuable. Just to feel the sun shine on your face or to have the wind blow through your hair is a win. To live is to win.

The devil really thought he had Christ beaten when he saw him nailed to that cross. Hell had a holiday and death did a jig when they saw the man Christ Jesus hanging on that tree. The angels stood mystified that they had not been called to battle. The moon blushed with shame, and the sun refused to shine its light upon so great an injustice. The earth mourned and sobbed so violently that it caused an earthquake. The disciples scattered like chaff thrown into the wind. The death of one so wonderful must have seemed to be such a defeat, such a great loss, the ultimate disaster, when God is dead.

Mary and the other women mourned. Joseph of Arimathea prepared Jesus' cold, dead body for the grave. The Roman soldiers mockingly stood outside his tomb, not to make sure he could not get out, but to make sure no one could go in. But what hell did not understand, what the grave did not understand, what the disciples did not understand, and what the devil did not understand is that **winners always win.**

Christ took the seeming loss on the cross and paid the price for the sins of lost humanity. After he had paid the price and purchased salvation with the sinless blood of the Lamb of God, he got up from the grave, having pulled victory out of the jaws of defeat.

Winners always win.

This is the ultimate comeback. He came back from the dead, and when he got up from the grave on that first Easter Sunday morning, he demonstrated for us that just by living against the odds, just by living in spite of the attack, just by the simple act of living, he won.

He won because the situation he was in was not strong enough to keep him down. He won because the circumstance of the Cross was not enough to stop him from completing the mission that God had placed him here to accomplish. He won because he is alive.

Christianity was born in a loss. All Christians must point back to the perceived loss on the cross and in that loss see that from that loss came our victorious lives in Christ. Even when Christ lost, he won. Because our God and King is a winner, and winners always win. Christ's death on the cross sure looked like a tragedy, but it turned into our triumph.

Evaluate your self-perception by marking how you see yourself on each scale below.

| 1 | 2 | 3 | 4 | 5 | 6 | 7 | 8 | 9 | 10 |

I was born to lose.   God created me a winner.

| 1 | 2 | 3 | 4 | 5 | 6 | 7 | 8 | 9 | 10 |

Life's trials hold me back.   Life's trials strengthen me for future battles.

| 1 | 2 | 3 | 4 | 5 | 6 | 7 | 8 | 9 | 10 |

I don't have what it takes to win.   God's grace has helped me win.

| 1 | 2 | 3 | 4 | 5 | 6 | 7 | 8 | 9 | 10 |

I've never been a winner.   Even my birth was a victory!

- How do you perceive yourself—as a winner, as a loser, or somewhere in between?

- How does your self-perception affect how you minister to students?

- How can you move closer to seeing yourself as a winner through God's grace?

chapter 4

anatomy of a loser

"As a dog returns to its vomit, so a fool repeats his folly" (Proverbs 26:11).

Just as winners always seem to find a way to win, losers always seem to find a way to lose. If you do not learn how to impart a winning spirit to losers, they will always lose. They will leave a trail of disappointment across the lives of their parents, friends, and youth workers. Losers will emerge out of good, strong, supportive family systems and still end up in divorce court. Losers will have positive socioeconomic underpinnings and still end up bankrupt and penniless.

You can put losers in winning situations, and they will still lose. Life can deal a loser a winning hand, and he or she will still find a way to lose. Losers can have the odds in their favor and still snatch a defeat out of the jaws of victory.

It doesn't matter where you put them or how strong their support systems are, losers are going to lose. Because their problems are internal and not external, they must first overcome their way of thinking before they can overcome their way of living. Losers are like the late Charles Schultz's *Peanuts* character Pigpen: They are surrounded by a cloud of defeat, and you can almost detect the stench of loss all around them. Until losers can be taught to unlock the winners inside their spirits, they will continue to carry the dark cloud of defeat. They must allow the wind of the Holy Spirit to blow the dark cloud away and the light of the fire of God to illuminate their vision (Acts 2).

the day of pentecost

On the day of Pentecost in the upper room, first the wind of the Spirit had to blow on the twelve souls who had assembled there. The wind had to blow on them to blow away the defeat, depression, and doubts of yesterday. Then they could be fully open to receive a fresh fire, fresh vision, and new passion from God. Then the tongues of fire sat on top of their heads, turning them into living candles that shone forth the light, power, and glory of God.

After they had been blown upon and then illuminated with this light from heaven, they had a change in their speech. They spoke with new tongues, and their ability to witness about the wonderful works of Jesus Christ was changed. They spilled out into the highways and byways of that great city, and their joy caused such an uproar that it looked like they were drunk. But they had received the new wine of the Holy Spirit, and under the influence of that Spirit, those simple people turned the world upside down.

I believe they received a winning spirit in that upper room, and through pain, rejection, and persecution they maintained that spirit until they had won people all over the world for the cause of Christ Jesus. They were losers before they got that spirit, so even the resurrected Christ told them they needed to wait until they got it. Even though they had the gospel and were buttressed with an intimate encounter with the risen Lord, they needed the Holy Spirit to blow and burn out the losers that were inside their psyche—their mind-set had to be changed before they could do any real and lasting good. Because losers always lose until they're changed and empowered by God, they can have the right information, but without the power or inspiration of God, there will be no lasting demonstration in their lives.

You can even put a loser in the White House, and despite an Ivy League education, the strongest financial support system, and access to the greatest Christlike council this side of heaven, a loser will still blow it every time.

trained to lose

Losers have been trained to lose. Often they have been raised into family systems that, despite perceived success and worldly acclaim, have internal cracks. Those cracks are hidden on the outside, but they produce children who feel like losers. Many teenagers who attend our suburban churches and live in the bedroom communities of America really believe they're losers. They live with parents who barely speak; they live in a materialistic society that places more value on things than on people. They feel like they're constantly being compared to the Joneses, and in their heart of hearts, despite access to money, education, and material goods, they feel like losers.

And because they feel like losers, they begin to act like losers. The good kids who come from good families and live in good communities start to do drugs. The average parent or youth worker can be taken aback by this selection of life path because these good kids have been taught to do better. But if the teenagers feel like losers, they will do almost anything to stop themselves from feeling that way. And if the feeling is not addressed, they will begin to self-medicate or act out in negative ways that will help them feel less like losers. When teenagers take drugs or abuse alcohol, they feel like the dark clouds that normally hinder their ability to speak out or dream out their own lives somehow dissipate.

Even the term *high* suggests that people who abuse substances to get high are subconsciously telling us that they feel so very low that they believe they're doomed to be lost in the depths of their own lives. This is a losing spirit, and this spirit can grow up in kids in the projects and housing developments of our urban centers; it can grow up on the beaches of the Caribbean; it can grow up in the posh neighborhoods of America's elite.

For some it is a crack pipe, for others it is one stiff drink too many, for some it is a line of cocaine, and for others it is a spoonful of heroin. We must reach our teenagers with a winning spirit. Parents, ministers, youth workers, and counselors must not allow stereotypes or prejudices to cause us to say that some teenagers need a winning spirit and others do not.

For even in the youth ministries of the great and affluent churches of this country—in many of which I have had the distinct privilege of praying with teenagers—there are teenagers who feel like losers in a cruel game called life.

gina's story

Early on in my ministry, I remember praying with an eighteen-year-old I'll call Gina. I had driven to one of the Ivy League schools in New England to preach for their Sunday night chapel services. It was, and still is, my custom to pray with and for any students who came up to the altar after the sermon. That night as I was praying for students, Gina came forward.

Gina was a beautiful Asian girl, dressed from head to toe in the latest European fashions. She was a 4.0 student at one of America's best schools. She'd driven to the chapel from her off-campus apartment in an expensive luxury automobile. She was popular and outgoing, and she seemed to be on the fast track to success. Her parents had come to America as immigrants and, through hard work and great focus, had managed to start a successful family business that now supported them and paid for all of Gina's education and expenses. Knowing all this, you might wonder why Gina would need prayer at all; certainly the poor kids in my youth church gladly would have traded places with her. But Gina had a secret. I don't know what it is about me that makes people feel comfortable about sharing their secrets with me, but I pray that I never lose it because so often **who we really are is all wrapped up not in our successes but in our secrets.**

One tear was flowing from one of Gina's almond-shaped eyes as I leaned my ear toward her head to find out what she wanted me to pray for. As she told me her life story—about her family and how she lived in front of people—I remember having the strongest feeling she was obfuscating her real issue. So I looked into her eyes and said, "But that's not it!" Instantly the tears began to flow and the real story came up out of her heart.

Gina was pregnant, again. She had a long-standing relationship with a boy who

Who we really are is all wrapped up not in our successes but in our secrets.

also went to the school, and he would stay in the relationship with her only if she gave herself to him sexually. She had always felt so alone and under so much pressure to perform academically that the idea of being alone and without him was too much for her to even consider. She wept because he, too, was from a good family and would be totally disgraced by the birth of a child out of wedlock.

He was standing in the back of the church, glaring at me as she cried. He was wondering what she was saying, paralyzed with fear that this man holding a microphone would soon know his secrets.

As she cried and talked, I heard her say through her tears that she had scheduled an abortion for that weekend but she was devastated because she had already had one baby and one abortion with this boyfriend, and the idea of going through the whole ordeal and then living with the guilt again was more than she thought she could stand.

I remember how God began to minister to her that night, from the rich well of his amazing grace. I told her how God's love was still available to her and even though she, through her own bad choices, had made a mess of her life and Christianity, Jesus could put the pieces of her life together again.

That night I had the opportunity to pray not only with Gina, but also with her boyfriend. They confessed their sins not only to God and to this meager preacher, but to their local pastor, who was then able to go on and guide them in their decision that night before the college chapel altar: to keep and raise their child.

That night I saw God take a gold-plated loser and turn her into a winner in an instant. I told Gina that God had given her a second chance and she now had the opportunity to shower all the love and care that was due the first baby on the child that God had graced her to bear. I told her that while she had a choice as to what she would do with the baby's life, God had a plan for the child and for Gina. I told her that she could not allow the mistakes of her past to hinder her from making a better decision for today. And through God's grace she heard me, and that night I believe that more than a baby was saved. I believe that the grace of God saved Gina, her boyfriend, and the baby.

This encounter taught me very early on in my ministry that I could not judge people from outward appearances, social status, or socioeconomic position. Each person has to grapple daily with life's struggles and temptations in our quest to be the winners God has ordained us to be.

Gina's parents in ignorance were raising a loser. They had provided a good home, a moral family, and a sound education, but somehow Gina had fallen into a losing cycle and was bound to be caught in it until God's grace pulled her out of the palace of her pain.

born to lose

Most losers believe in their hearts that they are born to lose and there is no real escape for them. Intuitively, they expect, predict, and then select a losing life choice that traps them in losing cycles. They walk around not totally committed to anyone or anything because they are waiting for the other shoe to drop, for the lights to come on, and for someone to yell, "Surprise!" They live always expecting the floor to fall in under their feet. Even when things are going great for losers, they live with the constant expectation that things will quickly come crashing down on their heads because they believe they were born to lose. Consequently and sadly, they are so busy waiting for things to go wrong that they do not have enough energy left to help things go right. They are trapped in a cycle of defeat.

Losers are not really born to lose; they simply believe they are born to lose, so they live their lives like they're going to lose, and they do lose.

Losers can sit with you for hours and rehearse for you all the tragedies, some truly major and others definitely minor, which have befallen them "all their lives." They will tell you at length about their friends and family members who have been trapped in losing situations, neighborhoods, family systems, or personal psychology and explain to you in graphic detail how they have somehow inherited this bad luck or family curse that now overshadows their destiny like a cloud of doom. **Losers are not really born to lose; they simply believe they are born to lose, so they live their lives like they're going to lose, and they do lose.**

transforming losers

Many preachers believe it is enough to lead losers to Christ, but they are sadly mistaken. If losers come to Christ expecting Christ to instantly make them into winners, the losers will only be disappointed in Christ and in his church—and, of course, the losers were expecting to be disappointed again anyway. Now for losers to expect Christ to just make them into winners would be like me expecting to be able to slam-dunk a basketball just because I'm wearing Shaquille O'Neal's Los Angeles Lakers team jersey. I have on the right jersey, but I am not Shaq.

Until we teach people how to put on more than the language and worship style of our brand of Christianity and we teach them how to put on Christ and truly step into a grace-walk with Christ, we are setting them up for pain and a level of "church-hurt" that can potentially turn them off to Christ. We are actually reinforcing their private, personal perceptions of themselves as losers. These expectations of losers will cause them to walk out of our red-hot, blowout church services, saying, "This Jesus stuff just doesn't work for me because I'm still a loser."

The youth pastor, pastor, counselor, or parent must go deeper than an ankle-high commitment to Christ and teach people how to swim out into their destinies by confronting the deep issues of their thinking. Until losers encounter people who have the winning spirit active and activated in their lives, they can be in the church but not have the church in them. They can find Christ but not experience the impact of the grace of God to shake the shackles of their thinking and self-perception. They can still be trapped in low self-esteem and dogged with the past errors of life before Christ.

What if the Apostle Paul had not had an encounter with the resurrected Christ? He certainly was caught in the losing cycle of persecuting a church that was destined to turn the whole world upside down. Paul was born a loser. Born into a nation that had lost its sovereignty and was living under the sole of the Roman boot. Paul had been well-educated but in a losing religious system that, while rich in wisdom and heritage, would fall into confusion with the fall of Jerusalem in the year A.D. 70.

Paul was a born loser. But on the road to Damascus while he was still caught up in the cycle of pain, persecution, and death, he had an encounter with the resurrected Christ. Jesus Christ is such a winner. Jesus won over the rule of Rome, for though a Roman governor, Pontius Pilate, sentenced him to death upon a Roman cross at the hands of Roman soldiers, Rome could not kill him. Christ triumphed over Rome. And even though he was buried, Jesus slipped the grip of death, shook off the sting of the death, and won victorious over the grave. Jesus had the winning spirit.

Jesus did not come to confront and defeat Paul, who was then Saul of Tarsus. No, Jesus came in the ninth chapter of Acts to convert Paul. And this one positive and powerful encounter threw Paul off the beast of his belief, blinded him to the system he had always known, and led him to the winning path. That encounter defined who he came to be and who we today celebrate as the chief apostle God used to write the greater part of the New Testament. God took someone who was born to lose and, by his grace, made him into a winner.

In the Scriptures we find this pattern of conversion evident from cover to cover. Moses was a loser until God's grace found him on the backside of the desert and made him a winner. Elisha was born a farmer and was destined to be a prophet, but he had to be impacted and empowered by the grace of God, in the person of Elijah. Elijah had the winning spirit, and after just one encounter with Elijah, Elisha began to press into the person he was destined to be. Can you imagine if these wonderful biblical characters had never had these life-changing encounters? Certainly they would not have left their mark on the world, nor would they be listed among the great heroes of holy writ.

Thanks to the Father of lights, that he is still raising up people all over the body of Christ who will light the path to personal freedom and private victory in the lives of his children. God is raising up people who are so filled with the winning spirit that people who get around them are being challenged to break out of their low self-esteem and poor self-image and to press into their true destinies in God.

If you never have had a relationship with a parent or a teacher or somebody who has this winning spirit, someone who has discovered the secrets of success that are locked up in the grace of God, if you never have had a relationship with somebody who challenges you to think beyond your situation and to begin to see the hand of God all around you and all inside your life, then chances are you will end up one of the poor people who grows up caught in the cycle of losing. You might even secretly believe you were born to lose, but you were not born to lose—you were born to win.

As you begin to accept winning as God's grace-gift to you, your self-view and then worldview will change, and you will see how you have been winning in life much more than you have ever been losing from the day you were conceived, not to mention the day you were born.

the suicycle

> "When Judas, who had betrayed him, saw that Jesus was condemned, he was seized with remorse and returned the thirty silver coins to the chief priests and the elders. 'I have sinned,' he said, 'for I have betrayed innocent blood.'
>
> " 'What is that to us?' they replied. 'That's your responsibility.'
>
> "So Judas threw the money into the temple and left. Then he went away and hanged himself" (Matthew 27:3-5).

Teenage losers are often brainwashed by life into believing that they are born to lose. Because they are pulled into this cycle of thinking, they slowly begin to believe that life has played some cruel joke on them and that God himself is against them. Sometimes losers decide that life is too terrible to continue, and thoughts of suicide begin to bombard them. This losing spirit is the kind of thing that causes young people to want to commit suicide. It causes people to turn to drugs or alcohol or anything that will arrest them from the doldrums of everyday life and transport them to some kind of temporary chemical paradise. They'll accept anything that will pull them from the pain of everyday living.

I call this the "suicycle." This is a cycle of loss that develops into a deep depression and causes teenagers to lose all hope, believing that life has betrayed them both painfully and permanently. These fatalistic feelings cause them to search for ways to escape daily life through substance abuse, sexual promiscuity, physical violence, or suicide.

Teenagers from any background can find themselves caught in the suicycle. The teenage girl who routinely binges and purges is on the same suicycle as the

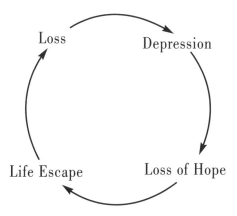

Loss → Depression → Loss of Hope → Life Escape → Loss

gangbanger who ritualistically performs drive-by shootings. They are two totally different people from two totally different worlds, but they are caught in the same cycle. They may live on opposite sides of the tracks, speak different languages, and have totally opposite family systems.

The teenage girl feels dominated by her parents. She feels like her two Christian parents are phonies. Her parents are publicly stable but privately troubled. She feels like she has lost all control over her own life and is a victim to the whims and winds of change that grip her parents. She feels powerless to change her situation, and she silently and secretly grows depressed. Behind a perfect smile, she begins to feel like a loser and to believe that God has turned his back on her. She decides to escape the situation, to exact some kind of control over the factors that have driven her into this depression. So she stages a juvenile coup d'état against this life she feels has betrayed her. She begins to deny her body its much-needed food. In an attempt to exercise control over something in her life, she threatens to end it.

The gangbanger feels like life has handed him a bad deck of cards, not to mention a raw deal. His father was incarcerated when he was born, and his mother was drug dependent. He is angry and depressed, and everything and everyone in his neighborhood has simply reinforced to him that there is no love or hope in this world. He doesn't actively seek to take his own life, but instead he puts himself in dangerous positions in which someone else might just take his life from him. The gang-related activity in itself is an attempt at suicide. His way of escape is a permanent and painful cycle of losing.

Other teenagers are simply raised by their parents to lose in life. And when a loser has raised you and you feel like you're caught in the cycle of losing, you must have some kind of encounter with somebody who calls you to your divine purpose. We as parents, pastors, and youth workers must make a positive and significant impact upon teenagers who find themselves caught in the crushing gears of the suicycle.

When teenagers meet the kinds of people who call them out of the suicycle and into a winning life, these people have such an impact on them. Even if the encounters are brief or decades past, people can always easily tell me the names of those positive people who pulled them out of the suicycle.

If you had a teacher who spoke to the winner in you, a counselor who spoke to the winner in you, a professor or a minister who spoke to the winner in you, just that one encounter is enough to turn the whole course of your life.

As I told you earlier, God graciously allowed me to have a moment with Redena, and in that moment God redirected the desires of her heart. Because Redena had been raised in a losing situation, the programming in her thinking process had been shaped by people who did not know how to win. Redena thought she needed a child out of wedlock, but all she needed was a winning spirit to enable her to see herself raising her children in another life that was better than the one she was living. In the safety of a pastoral relationship, I was able to inject a biblical viewpoint in an insane world. Praise God, she was able to come into a new way of thinking that liberated her to walk in her newness in Christ Jesus.

It is imperative that people who work with youth be armed with this kind of vision. The bulk of what we are called to do as mentors, leaders, ministers, pastors, and most important, parents is to impart truth to young people that will enable them to shake off the shackles of their past and press to the fullness of their purpose in Christ Jesus.

youth ministry insights

Below are ten steps that can help "losing" students change their thought patterns. Use these steps to guide an individual counseling session or to lead a group activity during a teaching time.

1. Think of the last major event in your life that made you feel like a loser.

2. Think of the attitude you had when you approached the event.

3. Did you apply yourself completely, or were you halfhearted?

4. Did you prepare physically, spiritually, and emotionally to the best of your ability for the event?

5. Were you shocked with the negative outcome, or did you expect to lose?

6. If you expected to lose, do you think your expectation affected your advance preparation? If so, how?

7. If you had an opportunity to go back in time and relive the event, what might you do differently?

8. Make a plan for the next time, based on your personal assessment of your previous performance.

9. Pray over your plan, and ask that God will give you the grace to execute the strategy you have selected.

10. Make a strong commitment to yourself that you will do your very best and give your all the next time you face that same challenge.

chapter 5

the making of a loser

"When Esau was forty years old, he married Judith daughter of Beeri the Hittite, and also Basemath daughter of Elon the Hittite. They were a source of grief to Isaac and Rebekah" (Genesis 26:34-35).

Recently I was speaking at a national convention for youth workers. After one of my sessions, a youth leader came up to me and, in the plain and honest speech of a youth worker, told me she had a youth group full of losers. While most of her teenagers were great kids, a large percentage of them were just losers. They were apathetic, lethargic, mean, and pathetic. They were neither from the inner city nor from failing families or communities, but they had a negative and aggressive outlook and were out of control. The church parents were irate with her and were just about to drive her out of the ministry at her church. She asked me very plainly, "Where do these kids come from?"

I shared with her three factors that I believe promote the development of losers:

- living in the shadow of the negative,
- the episodic worldview, and
- an easily fabricated identity.

Let's take a look at these three factors in the life of the biblical character Esau. Esau can give us some insight into the making of a loser, because in my mind Esau is the ultimate biblical model of a loser. If I ever write a Bible dictionary, a picture of Esau will be right beside my definition of a loser. Esau was the firstborn child, the heir and the favorite of his father, in a patriarchal society—and he still ended up a loser.

The Bible tells us that Esau was bested by his younger brother, Jacob. Esau first lost his birthright, which he sold to Jacob for a pot of spiced beans. Then later he lost his father's blessing in a case of mistaken identity.

The Scriptures tell us that Esau was so angry with his brother that he threatened to kill him and actually caused Jacob to run for his life. This, of course, only caused Jacob to increase his property, marry into the right family (when Esau married into a family system that was cursed, much to the chagrin of his parents), and return even more blessed. Without question Esau was a loser, and his life underscores these three factors that dramatically work to shape teenagers into self-described losers.

living in the shadow of the negative

I want to start in the middle of Esau's story because I believe the middle of the story tells us who he really is. Anyone can lose in the beginning; winners often lose the initial battles of their lives only to rally later and win the war. And some winners, like Napoleon, will even lose the last battles of their lives. But such defeats cannot really diminish their accomplishments when we study their lives in completed form. However, when you study what someone did after they suffered their first defeat, you'll gain some insight into who they are and how they will ultimately end up on the ledger of life.

After Esau sold his birthright to Jacob, he seems never to have gained control of the tailspin in his life. Esau never gained mastery of his destiny nor made the kinds of decisions that would have changed his mother's heart toward him or gained him the blessing of his father.

After he sold his birthright to his brother, Esau married one of the girls from the Hittite clans that surrounded his family. You must understand that God had told the descendents of Abraham that he would give them the lands of the people that lived in Canaan. Abraham had strictly forbidden his son, Isaac, from marrying into any of the families that lived in the land. Isaac had reached back into his own people to find Esau's mother, Rebekah, and so of course Esau's parents desired for their two sons to follow this same pattern and to avoid coming into marital covenant with people that God had promised to destroy.

In my sanctified imagination, I can hear Esau's parents chiding him about his interest in the local girls. They warned him in their talks around the cook fires and on camping and hunting trips in the wild. How many times did they tell that wild son of theirs that the local girls were not to be had as wives? How many times did the words of his parents tell him that God would not look kindly upon a union between a daughter of the Hittites and the seed of Abraham? And yet all these talks fell on deaf ears.

You would think that Esau, having already lost the birthright, would have been extra careful to hold on to the favor of his parents. You would have thought that Esau, who was comfortable on long treks and living in the great outdoors, would have welcomed a long overland journey to the land of his mother and would have gone and found himself an acceptable wife. But Esau exemplified the habits and decision-making that so often ensnare losers. He followed one bad decision with another, and at the very end of Genesis 26, he took two wives from the people of the land.

Scripture doesn't explain to us why he chose to live in the shadow of these negative women. Perhaps they were beautiful, perhaps they were wise; but Judith and

Basemath were from the wrong tribe and, therefore, a poor decision for the already wounded Esau. For him they were negative shadows that brought grief to both his father and his mother. And yet he did not relent nor repent until later on when he married a daughter of Ishmael (Genesis 28:9).

I have found that being surrounded by and then choosing to live in the shadow of negative people can be a factor that shapes into losers young people who should and can be winners.

The old adage that says you cannot walk with turkeys if you seek to soar with eagles is still true. Young people who surround themselves with negative peer groups can be so powerfully discouraged, derailed, and distracted by these negative people that they never emerge into the people God had graced them to become.

Parents and youth workers must work harder to show teenagers how much they are affected by their peer groups. We have to utilize statistics and case studies, biblical examples, and personal testimonies to show young people that the inner light of our destinies can be overshadowed by the dark shadows of negative friends or even family members.

It is imperative for teenagers to select Christian friends who are moral, directed, and positive. Today's teenagers are so influenced by their friends because in modern society they spend more time daily interacting with school friends than they do with their parents. All day they interact with their friends at school, only to go to the movies or the mall with the same set of friends on the weekends. Church and civic youth groups can help young people make positive connections by forming intentional social groups for our young people that are monitored, influenced, and led by positive adults.

If we aren't careful, modern technology will overwhelm our kids with negative influences that we cannot detect or monitor. In the past, most teenage girls had their heads permanently attached to telephone receivers, and all the parents had to do was pick up the other receivers and find out who or what their children were talking about. But now the Internet has created a global village for our kids that most parents can't enter or understand. The peer group has now gone high tech and is hiding in encrypted bits and bytes that fly along our telephone lines like crows in the night.

If a teenager's peer group is caught up in covert and negative activities, even the most concerned parent may be completely unaware of what is really going on in the life of the child.

Young men are clicking into pornographic or homosexual Web sites without their parents ever knowing; young girls are having virtual conversations with pedophiles who are camouflaged in chat rooms, pretending to be young teenagers. Technology is helping to make the negative shadow more intrusive and more covert as it seeks to overshadow our young people. And so we who have influence over young people have to give them all the information we can so they can be better keepers of their own souls. We must teach young people how and why they should avoid the negative shadows that seem to be everywhere. Sadly, even when young people are raised in positive homes, if they spend too much time in the shadow of negative people, they can fall into losing cycles and can take years to break out of them.

Both parents and youth must become aware, informed, and vigilant so teenagers can avoid those negative shadows.

the shadow of abuse

Esau chose to associate with negative people; he allowed his own desires to drive him into intimate relationships with people he had been expressly instructed to avoid. Esau is, in my mind, the worst kind of loser. He is the kind of loser who, through disobedience and shortsighted decisions, makes a shipwreck of his destiny. But another kind of shadow grips many of the teenagers who find themselves trapped in a cycle of losing. It is the shadow of abuse.

So many of today's youth have encountered abuse. Reported abuse, some researchers say, is more pervasive than ever. Perhaps because the stigma that was associated with reporting abuse has abated, more people are coming forward to seek help from counselors, pastors, police, and parents. The number of reported cases of physical, verbal, and sexual abuse is increasing every year.

The negative shadow of abuse is one of the strongest factors I have ever seen to trap young people in losing cycles. Abuse is not a shadow children select; it is not a product of peer group selection or a poor environment that a teenager chooses. It is a shadow that overpowers young people and drags them screaming into its lair. So we must take special time here to address it.

Carl was younger than six years old when his abuser started to attack him. His stepfather began to come into his room and abuse him before Carl ever was told that it was not right for another man to touch him in those places in that way. Carl grew up in that house under the shadow of secrecy, hiding his pain from a mother who chose to ignore what she knew was really going on because she was too afraid to face the truth and risk losing another man. Beguiled by his stepfather's false love and betrayed by his mother's denial, Carl grew to be a young man in that house.

For ten years Carl's stepfather raped both his body and his soul. By the time I met Carl, he already had run away from home and was living by his wits on the streets of the city. Sex to him was simply a commodity of exchange. Having never seen "normal," all he knew about was "abnormal." My pastor, Bishop T.D. Jakes, has taught me that abuse is simply "abnormal use," and indeed Carl had been used so abnormally that he thought abnormal was normal. He could barely believe that I didn't want anything from him or that my interest in him was purely Christian. Although he had been raised in a strict Christian home with all of the outward trappings of morality and church piety, the secret sins that ruled his home had left him church savvy but untouched. He could quote Scriptures but could not live them, and he honestly believed that no one else could either.

I remember getting a telephone call from him from the hospital after an enraged roommate had raped him again. I explained to Carl that he did not have to live that lifestyle anymore, that God's grace had given him a choice and the light of salvation had the power to make the shadows go away. I assured him that the way back was not easy but that it was far better than the lifestyle that now had him in its grip.

I remember him praying with me over the phone. He prayed without artifice or skill; with gritty and grimy honesty, he declared his need for God and came to Christ as he was. Christ accepted him without question or cost, without manipulation or exchange; Jesus paid it all.

I cannot tell you his was an instant transformation, for while I have seen teenagers instantly changed by the grace of God, Carl's is not one of those testimonies. His story, like most I have seen, required a slow and steady walk toward the light, and little by little, day by day, Carl crawled back to the destiny God had intended for him.

Today Carl is a happy and well-adjusted Christian man who ministers through God's grace, about God's grace, to people who have experienced sexual abuse. God's grace has now so healed him and pulled him from being a loser in life that he has enough of the winning spirit to share with others. Carl is a winner. God's grace empowered him to fight his way out of the shadow of his abuser and the abuse, to walk into the bright and beautiful light of life (Psalm 136; John 1:3-5) that is found in Christ Jesus. Carl has the winning spirit.

As a teenager I loved to watch wrestling. Not high school wrestling with its rules and regulations, but the campy and cheesy professional wrestling that was much less popular, less sexual, and less violent than the wrestling that dominates the hearts and minds of today's youth. Our wrestling was fun and innocent, with commercials for vitamins and saying your prayers—what can I say, it was a much lighter time.

My good friend Max and I would go down to the old Boston Garden on the green line subway trolley and scream our heads off over the good guys and boo the bad guys who gripped each other in figure-four leg locks or held each other in sleeper holds or tossed each other off the ropes and ring posts. We knew it was all fake, but it was all fun.

What I liked most about wrestling in those days was that the good guy always came back. The good guy was a hero, but not because he always won every fall in the match. He was a hero because even when the odds were against him and it looked like he was going to be down for the count, the good guy, whatever his name was, always knew his role and always fought his way back.

Max and I would cheer and jump and spill popcorn on the heads of the people with money who could sit closer to the ring than our balcony seats.

For teenagers to fight back from living in the shadow of abuse, whether sexual, verbal, or physical, takes a supreme act of courage. **Their fight is not fake, but through the grace of God, it is fixed.** Over two thousand years ago, Jesus Christ paid the price for their victory, and by his stripes they are healed from the prison and prism of their pain. Not only can they be released from the pain of their past; they can be so utterly changed that they no longer see life, God, or other people through a worldview colored by that pain. God can release them not only from the prison of the past but from the prism.

Their fight is not fake, but through the grace of God, it is fixed.

When counseling young people who have experienced abuse, I remind them that, like the wrestlers of old, the good guy may get bloodied and bashed around. The good guy might even get picked up and completely thrown out of the ring, but the good guy always wins.

I have tried to remind them over and over again, even as I reminded Carl, that they are the good guys, that they did not bring abuse upon themselves, nor are they at fault in any way. There is never an excuse for abusing a child of God. I remind them that, because Jesus has already purchased the outcome, their job is to stay in their role and fight for the victory. With Jesus, the good guy always wins.

episodic worldview

Before I allow Esau to slip from under the stem of my mental microscope, I must also point out the thought process of this big loser. Esau had a Polaroid-camera mind-set instead of a video-camera mind-set. His picture of reality was accurate but temporal.

He could only catch hold of the second and had no ability to examine life in its totality. This episodic worldview sees life only as a pronounced "now" instead of an ever-flowing and constant experience. This was the genesis of Esau's failure. This episodic worldview caused him to see the tree but miss the forest, to see the wave but miss the ocean, and to see the period but miss the sentence.

All Esau knew was that he was hungry right then. So he sold his future for temporary satisfaction. This factor is archetypal of losers. **They not only embrace the now, but they also disgrace the future.** Losers like Adam and Eve not only eat the fruit; they curse the future for themselves and anyone else who will be depending on them to have made the right decisions.

Esau traded something invaluable for a pot of beans. This was the height of idiocy. Many people will laugh at poor old Esau, but let's take the time to examine our own lives and see how many times we have settled for a temporary pleasure that we knew was wrong and shortsighted, rather than waited for a right and seemingly tardy solution. How many times have we driven faster and risked the ticket? neglected to study and cheated on the exam? called in sick and went on to have some fun adventure? Deep inside each of us is a little Esau, screaming to come out and ruin our lives.

They not only embrace the now, but they also disgrace the future.

The episodic worldview can cripple teenagers. Today's teenagers are, first of all, too young to have much inward perspective, which is formed by evaluating personal experiences. And they are often so unfamiliar with world history or family history that they have very little outward perspective. That is perspective informed by the study of how time affects people and their lives.

To the modern teenager, time is such a mystery because those of us who have become the experts on time's effects are seldom honest about the genesis of our decisions and how they have affected our lives.

Few parents openly share with their teenagers how premarital sex affected their lives, so teenagers have no real perspective on it and often make episodic decisions instead of the long-looking decisions their parents would like them to make. When parents tell their children about sexually transmitted diseases or unwanted pregnancies that plagued them when they were young, the effect is very often the opposite of what most parents believe it will be. Instead of simply taking their parents' failures as excuses to also fail, mature teenagers respect their parents as truth tellers who can stand as firsthand witnesses of what episodic thinking can do.

Parents who show their children their tenth-grade report cards, even though they are littered with failing grades, and in graphic detail describe how poor study habits have affected their lives do not open themselves to ridicule from their teenagers but open their children up to the perspectives of the parents.

For that matter, pastors or youth workers who open up their past failures to the teenagers in their churches or youth groups give their students an oral history that can help inform them of what time can do with a bad decision. Youth workers must first gain permission from church leadership before they get transparent with youth because most modern parents feel that their cherubic teenagers are simply too innocent to know the honest truth. But today's teenagers, like Britney Spears, are "not that innocent" and could stand a good dose of the truth.

Parents who do not want their teenagers to think about life in an episodic manner must begin to give their kids the whole story:

"I don't want you to sleep around because I did and got pregnant as a teenager and never recovered!"

"I don't want you to have a boyfriend because I don't want you to lose your virginity at a young age like I did."

"I don't want you to drink because I did, and it almost ruined my whole life."

We adults tend to give speeches rather than tell narratives. Our teenagers are best taught even as Jesus taught us, through parables—the parables of our own lives and family histories.

My Uncle Robert was an alcoholic. He was perhaps the most brilliant man I have ever met in my life. His mind could process any concept faster than a computer. He was well-versed in music, French cuisine, art, and history. He was handsome and outgoing and had the kind of electric personality that started the party going and made everyone instantly either hate or adore him. My Uncle Robert was a relentless soul about everything he did. He had made, without a high school diploma, his first million dollars before he was forty years old. I loved him and respected him, but he was an alcoholic.

He was good to me. He loved his children and adored my mother and his own. But he, like his father before him, my grandfather, was an alcoholic. As life would have it, just when he had conquered his addiction, his body betrayed him. As a result of his years of abuse during his misspent, hellbent years in the sixties and seventies, he dropped dead during the nineties.

I remember sitting at his funeral service in a black and white suit, behind my mother, his sister, and thinking of how stupid and pointless was his death. I promised myself that night that I would never take a strong drink. Not because I was a Christian or because I had been raised not to, nor because I was a rising young preacher in our community. In that moment, none of those reasons, although they were all good, held much gravity. My Uncle Robert was dead, and all those other reasons to avoid strong drink evaporated from my mind like the morning dew in the Texas noonday sun. I made that decision that day for one reason: because it was too likely that I would be like most of the men in my family and get addicted to the stuff. I do not drink alcohol today—not because I don't like the stuff but because I am afraid that I will like it.

The story of Robert's life successfully canceled the episodes of anyone enticing me to ever drink alcohol again.

I have built my sermons on these same life stories. The teenagers who have lined church pews and school halls over the years have heard in graphic detail about the people who have wandered in and out of my life. The Scriptures are almost brutal in their honesty, and I have labored to be as honest. Year after year, God's grace has reached many young people through these simple stories. Many young people have made decisions not only to live out their faith, but also to live past the episodes and to protect their futures.

Sometimes to impart the winning spirit, we must examine how others have lost in that church, family, or community. That way, teenagers can really understand the impact of every decision and how time can really affect a decision over the course of a lifetime.

In military academies across the globe, historians are training soldiers with what they need to know to win. They not only train them by teaching the strategies of victorious generals; they also train them by showing the strategies of the vanquished.

easily fabricated identity

Let's allow Esau to slink off the witness stand as we call his brother, Jacob, to come forward and tell us about how he stole his brother's blessing. The birthright was purchased—through trickery, but still purchased. The blessing, on the other hand, was stolen. Jacob's mother concocted his venison stew. Jacob, with his clothes and a little special effects, fooled his father into giving him his brother's blessing.

It has always been interesting to me that all the proofs of Esau's identity were external. The taste and smell of the food, the feel of his arms, and the smell in his clothes were the hallmarks of his personhood.

Nothing in his character, nothing in his conversation, no private joke or secret shared between father and son, could distinguish him from his brother. I know that Jacob was wrong to steal his brother's identity, but I really believe that Esau's identity was too easy to steal. It seems as though there was no depth to his person, as though he was known only by what he could do, not for who he was. People who are known only by what they do are easy to replace with anyone who will supply that same service.

One of the strongest tendencies of losers is that they have no identity. Losers have no character; they become whoever the situation dictates them to be. There is very little to distinguish them from others. They want to dress like everyone else, live like everyone else, and drive like everyone else. They are easily fabricated and are simply manufactured in the factory of life. This is not because they do not have potential but because they are too afraid to be different.

As teenagers they drink because everyone else does, they party because everyone else does, and at church, sadly, they walk up to altars and recite prayers because everyone else does. They are the interchangeable people and personalities who walk lock step through life. They have not decided to be the masters of their own destinies, living each day in and by the grace of God. They have found their comfort zones and chosen to stay put. **Rather than be champs, they have chosen to be chumps. They are ordinary not by design but by resign.**

They have thrown their king's piece down on the chessboard of life before they have even lost a pawn, because they are more afraid to try and then lose than they are to just lose. They have resigned themselves to be ordinary. We can really know them only by what they do, not by who they are, for they will never show us who they are. Losers are too afraid to have real opinions or to voice original thoughts. Their episodic mind-set limits their ability to have a wider vision. They are blown around by every wind of doctrine, they are slaves to every fashion, and they have no inward brilliance that they seek to polish.

> Rather than be champs, they have chosen to be chumps. They are ordinary not by design but by resign.

If you show me teenagers who are not working to develop their character, then I will show you teenagers who are a clash of clichés and trite expressions they have adopted but not proved and who are heading to a place I call the "losers' circle."

The losers' circle is not a place for winners who have tried and failed. It is a place where losers go because they have not even tried to win. This circle is not a cycle, because a cycle suggests a progression of some sort. No, this is a circle without fence or wall, in which losers rest from their rest and grow more lethargic in the process. The losers' circle is for those people who have not sharpened their character through winning and losing, have learned nothing about themselves by standing on the shoulders of God's grace in the dark and lonely hours. The winners' circle is for all who have heard the gun and started their run; the losers' circle is for those who shook off their numbers and hailed a cab.

Winners are hard to find, but a loser can be replicated in an afternoon.

A young man came to my house one rainy night. My only son was still toddling around his room, throwing his toys into his toy box in preparation for the next day's toils of coloring with crayons and finger painting for the whole half a day at nursery school. I don't like to yell at people in front of my son, unless I'm preaching, and because I knew this young man's situation, I knew I would be yelling.

So we climbed into my SUV. I shifted into four-wheel drive and shot down the highway. What the young man had discovered about himself, thank God not too late, was that he had no character. That he had allowed abuse and denial to shape him into a human chameleon who could conform publicly into anything his audience required, only to lapse into great confusion when no one else was around to define his role. He had discovered that he was less than a man, less than a human, and he wanted to change.

After I finished yelling at him, like a marine sergeant in a war zone, I began to define *character* to him. I said, "*Character* is who you really are when no one is around. It is who you are when the lights go off; it is the base of your being and the defining principle by which you run your life." I told him to list for me the five things he liked most about himself, things that did not have to do with other people.

He gave me one defining characteristic, and I charged him to begin to build a frame of identity upon which he could begin to build the house of his own character, absent of people, internal and not just external, introspective and not just subjective.

During the following days, we talked about his character. I monitored his external activities and directed him to some in-depth Christian counseling. As the days turned into months, the boy I yelled at in my truck that night turned into a man I could talk to as a brother. He was more than a fabrication; he became the real article.

Losers are so easily replicated because they have no real identity. Their character is occluded by their desire to fit into the pack and to go with the flow. Winners, however, are not afraid to swim against the tide. They assert their identities, and they stick to their own moral compasses. The winds of popular opinion do not blow them about. More often than not, their strong stance for what they believe, whether stoic or outstanding, tends to influence the thinking of other people.

youth ministry insights

Below are three questions that will help someone grow beyond a negative experience and stretch into health and development. Use these in counseling young people who have experienced any of the factors that go into the making of a loser.

- What is the worst thing that has ever happened to you?

- What makes this event worse than anything else in your life?

- Based on Romans 8:28, what are three good things that were produced in your life as a result of this worst event in your life?

the making of a winner

"So Samuel took the horn of oil and anointed him in the presence of his brothers, and from that day on the Spirit of the Lord came upon David in power. Samuel then went to Ramah" (1 Samuel 16:13).

The life of King David is a wonderful backdrop for our conversation about winners. David will walk with us throughout the remainder of this book because he is a wonderful example of somebody who was born to lose but destined to win.

It seems everyone is enthralled with young David and his encounter with Goliath. Books have been written and great sermons have been preached about how David, armed only with his shepherd's sling, bested the giant Philistine on the field of battle. It is a great biblical story that can give hope to every underdog who has ever faced insurmountable odds and yet dared to believe that he or she could win.

In the theater of our imagination, we can still see David, the handsome, ruddy-faced lad, standing defiantly in front of the hideous-looking Goliath. The story is so powerful because it reminds all of us that when God is for us, no one, regardless of the person's strength or ability, can stand against us. David's victory causes us to believe that we can defeat the giants that stand against us in the battle of life and reminds us that the bigger they are, the harder they fall.

becoming a winner

I, like most preachers, love the Goliath and David account. But I am not as fascinated with his encounter with Goliath as I am with all that went into preparing David for his encounter with Goliath. Despite his obvious youth, David did not come to this encounter ill-prepared. A number of events that preceded his Goliath encounter, I believe, prepared him to step into that historic moment and to emerge a victor. This preparation, this system of personal development, that came before his encounter with the giant of the Philistines, warrants our close examination because it tells us what and how to become a winner, even when life has handed you a raw deal. We must understand the making of a winner. We must know how to make winners if we are charged with teaching teenagers in losing situations how to win. Not that we ourselves are manufacturing these winners; we are given the opportunity to introduce these teenagers to the grace of God, and through his grace they are changed from losers to winners.

Before David encountered the champion of the Philistines, he had already championed issues in his own life. Until you have overcome and been converted in your own thinking, you'll never be able to overcome the giants you encounter. And until you have overcome those personal giants, you will be unable to help anyone else overcome his or her own giants.

Sadly, today our churches are littered with people who, though they have memorized many neat sermons and have attended wonderful PowerPoint presentations and are well-informed about the work of Christ, have not allowed Christ to work on them. We will remain open to the attack of these giants until we allow God to impact our thinking. You can go to all the meetings, all the churches, and all the counseling you want to, but until you have been impacted in the way you think and live and move and respond to negative stimuli, you will find yourself falling into the same patterns of losing.

> We can and must be made into winners, and we need personal encounters with other winners if we are to reach our potential.

I believe that winners can be made. I believe that all of us are born to be winners. I also believe that all of us can overcome any losing situation life throws at us. But I also believe all of us need other people to help shape us into the victorious "overcomers" God intends for us to be. **We can and must be made into winners, and we need personal encounters with other winners if we are to reach our potential.**

I believe that we all need a coach or a number of coaches who can call us to our highest good and remind us that God still has a greater grace for those who are mindful that they are in need of his divine favor. Coaches come not only to train us how to win, but also to hold us accountable to our highest purpose. They come to remind us that mediocrity is never an option and that striving for our personal best is the only way to discover our highest good.

the sheepfold experience

The sheepfold was the place God used to train and coach David. While he was yet a shepherd boy, long before he had heard the trumpet blow a call to battle or the women had placed his name in their epic songs, David was getting ready for his giant. Maybe he knew a day was coming that would define his life and fix his destiny; perhaps there was an early twinkling in his eye, or the flapping butterflies of foreshadowed potential told him a day was coming that would make him a historic figure.

Or perhaps he never imagined that his life would turn from one thing to the next. Perhaps he had just decided to be the very best shepherd he could be, and in that faithful and fate-filled service, he somehow attracted the favor of the God of Israel. On this point the Scriptures are silent and so we, too, must remain silent, not knowing if David knew that with one encounter with Samuel—David's first coach—his whole life course would change.

The sheepfold taught David how to be responsible and how to rely on God. The sheepfold taught David the value of the shepherd, and the sheepfold taught David the value of one sheep.

All of us need a sheepfold experience. It is the first stone on the road to becoming a winner. It is the place where we learn personal mastery; the place where we discover that if we work hard at something, we can make a difference in some small way. The sheepfold for a teenager may be his or her first part-time job or baby-sitting position. It may be found in a paper route or in simply fulfilling a list of daily household chores. It may be found in the daily assignment to milk the cows, to walk the dogs, to slop the hogs, or to gather the fresh hen eggs. It might be in changing the Kitty Litter or putting new paper down in the birdcage. It may be starting the cars in the morning and backing them out of the garage or shoveling the walk clear of the heavy winter snow.

The actual makeup of the sheepfold experience really has no bearing. This experience happens in a controlled environment in which the teenager can begin to feel the impact of his or her existence upon other living beings. The sheepfold is the place where self-image begins to take its form.

David might not have been very important to his older brothers, but he certainly was important to those sheep. Jesse would not have gone bankrupt if David lost one of the sheep with which he had charged David. So the loss of a sheep's life probably was not the end of the world for David's father. But the loss of life would have been a lot more important to the sheep. The sheepfold experience should teach us that others are counting on us to perform. Although the total weight of the whole family or operation was not on David's narrow shoulders, he did have to shoulder the responsibility for the food and safety of his flock.

So the sheepfold gave David responsibility and accountability but also had enough of a margin for error that he had the space to fail and still wind up a winner. Certainly no boy who uses a sling masters the sling in one day. No, it was through practice and constant use that the boy learned how to use the weapon of the shepherd. He learned that discipline in the relative safety of the sheepfold, before he needed it to defeat the giant.

a controlled environment

When making winners, or when training losing teenagers how to win, you must place the young people in a controlled environment in which they can discover that they can win. The sheepfold experience should not consist of a critical leadership position upon which a family or organization is totally dependent; the sheepfold experience should be a controlled environment in which failure is survivable.

After school each day my seven-year-old son, Christopher, is assigned to walk our dog. Lady, our family dog, is a purebred bouvier des Flandres, and at two years of age, the dog outweighed my son by seven pounds. At times I would look out the back windows of our house and see Lady dragging my lanky seven-year-old name-sake all around the back yard as Christopher attempted simply to hold onto her leash. I would wonder who was really walking the other, the dog or the boy.

But the system works because Lady really has no intention of running away from home and is quite an expert at eliminating her own waste. So why do I have him walk a dog that will walk itself? I am really just using the experience to help teach my son how important his contribution is to the family and to our family dog. The whole thing is a sheepfold experience for him. This experience also gives me an opportunity to shower him with praise. I praise my son for fulfilling his responsibility and for giving an accurate account of how and where Lady relieved herself. I praise him for being a good dog owner and for taking care of his duty before he runs into his room and fires up his computer game system. When he forgets to walk the dog, I use it as an object lesson and re-emphasize the importance of his role.

One day he will realize what I have been doing, but I pray it will be too late and he will have already developed a strong idea of how much power he has to impact and influence the lives and feelings of others.

As I study the book of Genesis, I begin to think that the only reason a sovereign and all-powerful God placed Adam in the Garden of Eden and commanded him to work and keep the garden was to provide his son Adam with a sheepfold experience. God put Adam in a controlled environment with fresh food and water and with wild animals that lived under his dominion. God certainly had the power to run and keep the Garden from heaven, but instead he decided to trust the task to Adam. Now you must also consider that God had all foreknowledge and so he entrusted the task of keeping the Garden and avoiding the tree of knowledge of good and evil, having full knowledge that Adam would blow the whole thing. So Scripture tells us that before he had even made Adam, in eternity past, Jesus Christ had already decided to be the sacrificial lamb who would pay for Adam's failure in the Garden.

God simply could have made it impossible for Adam to have access to the forbidden fruit, but instead he chose to allow Adam to exercise responsibility and accountability. Like all dutiful fathers, God had already decided to pay the price for any of the damage his son's poor decision-making might have caused. I believe the Garden of Eden was a sheepfold experience designed to teach mankind how to be responsible and to have a sense of mastery over the incredible creation that God had made with the words of his mouth here on the earth.

the broken fall

If we take this concept to the next step, you can begin to see that the fall of humans in the Garden of Eden was in and off itself a sheepfold experience. Yes, humans were allowed to fall, but before we could fall completely away from the loving grasp of the Father, Jesus came to break our fall.

A few summers back, I took a group of my youth church's missionaries on a trip to the mountains. When we pulled up to the foot of the mountain, my many inner-city-born young people marveled at why I would want them to climb up a mountain. I told them that the mountain would teach us valuable lessons about ourselves and about our God as we climbed to the summit. I told them that, but I really had no idea how well it would teach us.

We had been on the rock face for less than half an hour when one of our less-experienced climbers lost footing and began to spin out of control down the side of the mountain. I had taken a steeper path to the summit so that I could watch over some of our more adventuresome climbers, so I was not with the group of students teamed up with the climber who was caught in the fall. But Christy was.

Christy was a little altitude-sick that morning, so even though she was a strong climber and wanted to tear up the uncharted path with the daredevils, I had directed her to stay with the group that was coming up the beaten path to the summit, to make sure everyone would be covered and accompanied by a strong partner. When Christy, a stately blond-haired, blue-eyed beauty, saw her fellow climber careening out of control down the side of the mountain, she did not hesitate a moment. She threw herself down upon the body of her fellow climber and broke the climber's fall, saving the climber from serious injury.

Likewise, Jesus Christ saw all humanity careening out of control down the rock face of eternity. He threw himself down from the safety of heaven and against the body of fallen humanity and broke our fall. It was his grace that kept us from falling completely down to our destruction, and it will be his grace that will put us back on the right path and then lead us safely to the highest point of our potential.

The fallen climber told me and the rest of our team the story, and I reminded the group that I had told them the mountain would teach us a great life lesson. Because the fall had been broken, the climber had suffered no real damage except for a few cuts and bruises. The climber was fine and was able to successfully complete the climb. When I heard about the minor cuts and bruises, the motivator on the inside of me stood up. I told the young people on the side of that mountain, **"Even though you sometimes get a flesh wound, you must always keep on climbing."**

When God's grace saves your life but the fall still wounds your flesh, don't worry.

"Even though you sometimes get a flesh wound, you must always keep on climbing."

Thank God that all you have is a flesh wound, press through the pain of your flesh, and press on toward the summit of your success. God would not have caught you if you were destined to lose. Keep climbing, because the fact that grace grabbed you is a clear indication that you can win if you don't give up.

Youth workers, counselors, pastors, and parents who are seeking to teach teenagers how to win must help create sheepfold experiences and provide gardens of grace. In these controlled and monitored environments, we can teach our teenagers. They can learn in a safe and controlled environment the power of their contribution to the world. We must allow them to spread their wings, but we must always be able to reach out and pull them back to the rock that we are clinging to. That rock is Jesus.

youth ministry **in**sights

Follow these seven practical steps to help the teenagers in your group see themselves as winners through God's grace.

1. Pray for your youth group.

2. Study the obstacles that your young people have already faced.

3. Find Bible characters that correspond with the situations and obstacles your youth are facing.

4. Study the faith bridges that carried these biblical characters over their obstacles.

5. Begin to teach, preach, and counsel your teenagers from these Bible studies.

6. Create opportunities within your youth ministry to introduce the "bridge" factors into the lives of your students.

7. Downplay or completely eliminate all ministry functions that do not impart these "bridge" factors. Reshape existing ministry activities to intentionally impart these factors.

chapter 7

the prophetic coach

"So Samuel took the horn of oil and anointed him in the presence of his brothers, and from that day on the Spirit of the Lord came upon David in power. Samuel then went to Ramah" (1 Samuel 16:13).

sam i am

The Scriptures record for us that the shepherd boy David was anointed by the great prophet Samuel. I believe that this encounter with the old and wizened prophet of Israel was for David the defining moment of his life. It was at that moment that his identity clapped hands with his destiny. This encounter was the defining moment when the shepherd boy was informed that although he was overlooked by his father and was the least of his brothers, he had not been overlooked or discounted by God. This memory must have formed a solid bedrock in the psyche of David. An important and powerful man of God had stepped into his life and told him that one day, if he walked with God, he would be somebody. This was just a brief moment in the history of David the shepherd, but it was the first inauguration of David the king. We who work with teenagers must not miss this moment or allow the circumstances that define our young people's lives—whether they be economic, societal, or familial—to deter us from believing that we can have a profound impact on the lives of our teenagers in just the brief moments we have with them.

Many youth workers and counselors have shared with me their desire to take their young people into their homes. Or they have lamented that they were not able to just pull their youth out of the negative systems and situations that they were born into. I have to bring David back into the center of their minds so they can see how much impact one positive person can have on a negative situation.

In mathematics when a positive number is added to a negative number, the total of those numbers is either negative or positive. This outcome is dictated by whether the positive number is greater than the negative or the negative number is greater than the positive. The miracle of Christlike mentorship is that if the Holy Spirit is active in the life of the parent, youth leader, or counselor, the Holy Spirit is always greater than the negative influences that are active in the life of the teenager. Despite how negative the situation is, God's power is always greater and is always positive.

David had a brief encounter with a positive person. That one short encounter with a positive person—even though Samuel was from outside David's family system—was enough of an influence to begin to help David become a winner.

Samuel came not as a father or as a brother; he came as a coach. The job of the coach is to identify the true position of a player and to help the player fulfill that role on the team. The coach is not on the field of play. The coach uses that perspective as a partial observer to help players improve their actions within the scope of the game.

Young people need spiritual coaches. They need partial observers who earnestly care about their lives and outcomes. They need coaches who have spent enough time praying for them and getting to know them on a practical level that the coaches have both divine and personal perspective on the gifts, talents, and potential of young people.

Coaches speak, then, not only to the actions of the young people they nurture, but also to the future actions their teenagers will one day achieve. Coaches see through the eyes of divine hope and speak prophetic words of destiny over the lives of their teenagers. Sometimes coaches speak not from what they see in young people but from what they believe by faith in God they will see manifested in the lives of young people.

my coaches

I have been blessed with many coaches. When I was a child, the old mothers of the church that I grew up in started to call me "Preacher." I was seven months old when my mother started to bring us to that storefront church on Dudley Street in Boston, and when the preacher really got going in his sermon, I had the tendency to start talking back to him.

Now you must be familiar with the strange and wonderful symmetry of the African-American pulpit to understand the powerful chemistry between the speaker and the audience during a sermon in the tradition of church that I grew up in. In the black church, the preacher does not preach alone, nor is the sermon some flat soliloquy; but like some Greek drama of old, the church becomes a chorus that echoes and responds to the pitch, tone, and tenor of the speaker. Like a strange symphony, the voices blend together in a crescendo of power and praise.

It was in this atmosphere that I found my voice, my preaching voice. Though my words had no clear meaning to adult listeners, and though my mother would have fits trying to keep me quiet, the older women of the church—whom we called "the mothers"—would smile knowingly and say that I was just preaching along with the speaker. They would remark on my timing, my excitement, and my joy. Without a doubt, they began to call me "Preacher." And the name stuck. My little Sunday school buddies started calling me Preacher (and some still do to this day), and the younger church members started calling me Preacher. People began to hold me to a higher level of expectation as I made my Sunday school recitations or recited my little Scriptures because one day I would preach. When we would play Church on the front porch, I would always pretend that I was the preacher.

And today what I used to pretend to be, I now am. I cannot say that I am a preacher because those church mothers said I would preach or that they had some deep spiritual insight that no one else had or that they could see some call on my life that was undetected by most of the people who may have seen just an overactive and somewhat distracting baby making too much noise in church. All I can say is that I am glad they did not call me "Stupid." I am glad they did not call me "Nuisance" or "Big Mouth." They did not sneer at my outbursts but only smiled and nodded knowingly at each other like they shared some secret that no one else could know.

Mother Lucile "Lady" Jefferson would look at me through her big glasses and say through a serious smile, " Preacher, you know that one day you are going to preach the gospel." And I would smile back and say, "Yes, Ma'am, one day!"

Most of those mothers have gone on to reap their great heavenly reward, but even today at times, when preaching a real good sermon to a responsive congregation, I can almost imagine them leaning down over the golden banisters of heaven's great porches and, with silken handkerchiefs waving frantically in their hands, saying, "Preach, Preacher." I am living their words today.

The church mothers became for me great coaches. They would check my report cards and give me extra dollars for good grades, because they believed that a preacher needed to be smart. They would watch over me in church to make sure that I behaved, because they believed that a preacher needed to have good self-control. The mothers always had a word of encouragement, and even when I felt like taking my time and talents into some other field of engagement, they would remind me of the call on my life to preach.

I am thankful to God that because I started to preach at such a young age, all of those mothers did live to see me preach. I can see Mother Catherine Dorsey's face as she watched me deliver my first sermon. I often wonder if she really knew how much of an influence she had on my life. Her words and the words of all those beautiful church mothers created a feeling of destiny and expectation inside of me. Their positive words formed a framework for my life.

Even today I wonder if they can see me and if they are watching me. That thought always causes me to recheck my commitment and to reset my resolve. I want them to be proud of me, and so even in death they are still coaching. They call me to play my role on the team better and to fulfill my position with all the grace that God has given me. They also cause me to shake off thoughts of quitting or shrinking back from the challenges that confront me. Perhaps because they believed in my calling so completely, I am still buttressed by the strength of their belief.

you are sam

Every child needs a coach. Every parent is a coach—someone who can see through the eyes of prayer and with divine perspective can see the grace of God in the life of a teenager and then call that child to greatness. Every youth worker has to see and know each and every teenager not by his or her flesh or by outward actions but by the Spirit. We have to see beyond teenagers' actions and believe God will activate the greater potential that teenagers have lying dormant inside. **Only the Holy Spirit can give us this type of insight, this prophetic vision, but if there are no prophets (coaches) to see the potential, there will be no Davids (players) to receive the anointing.**

Every youth leader should begin to see himself or herself as a Samuel who is called to anoint Davids. Every youth leader must stop thinking of himself or herself as just on the side of ministry, a spiritual baby sitter who is dispatched from the church in order to occupy the time of the children. Leaders must stop thinking so lowly of the position that God has called them to. Youth leaders need to see themselves as the prophetic seers set in the house of God, even see themselves as the Samuels who are called to anoint and to speak positively over the lives of the young people of whom they have been given charge.

> Only the Holy Spirit can give us this type of insight, this prophetic vision, but if there are no prophets (coaches) to see the potential, there will be no Davids (players) to receive the anointing.

Parents no longer should think of themselves as outside the youth ministry. In fact, when someone becomes a parent, that person has just been called into real youth ministry. Parents are called to prayerfully stand on the front line of all great youth ministries. God has called parents to pray and prophesy over their children. God has called them to anoint their children to be leaders, to be excellent, to be part of God's salvation plan for the earth. Parents may not have horns of oil, but they can anoint and submerge their children with effectual fervent prayers (James 5:16). When parents realize that their role is more vital than the youth worker's, we will begin to see young people who are being empowered with a winning spirit.

parents are coaches too

Parents are called to pastor and train their children to go to the highest level in Christ Jesus. Parents are the spiritual Samuels set as priests and prophets in their homes. When parents are activated and youth workers are simply reinforcing the truths and tenets that are being taught in the home, then we begin to see generations of Davids arise within a church.

Sadly, the teenagers who line the padded pews of our churches today are in a weakened state because not enough parents see themselves as the spiritual Samuels set in their homes. But there is enough blame for all of us to share responsibility for the sad spiritual health of today's teens. We cannot lay this all on the shoulders of parents. Youth workers, pastors, and counselors have to stop just dispensing powerless counsel or just speaking to the psychological issues that pervade today's youth culture, while we miss ministering to the real heart issues in the lives of our real teens.

Our young people really don't need anybody else to do just another psycho-profile or to fill their heads with more psychobabble. They will not be helped by the reams of statistical analysis that we compile only for our educated to debate. Our scholarship is necessary, our counsel is important, but let us not simply study the disease and give no thought to bringing teens to the cure.

If we do, we are just lurking like roaches through the darkness trying to pick up the crumbs of understanding off the floor of their collective psyche, when God is calling us to turn on the light and to dispel the darkness. The roaches are just looking for the next tiny tidbits of knowledge while our young people are being swallowed up in the darkness that is overwhelming today's youth culture.

Samuel did not deal with the reason Jesse, David's father, did not invite David to the sacrifice. He did not ask who David's mother was or why David had been given responsibility over the sheep. The prophet didn't deal with the past at all. Instead, in this brief encounter, he set David's focus completely on his future. The prophet spoke not to David's lowly location; he spoke only to his destination. Samuel was not deterred by the smell of the sheep; he covered that smell with the sweet smell of the anointing oil. And that smell was enough to make David know that while he had started in the pasture, he would end up in the palace.

I am not discounting the validity of counseling and the need to examine the past systems of thinking that may have worked to trap young people in losing cycles, for I have spent half my ministry life doing crisis counseling with teenagers. I believe counseling has a real and necessary role in the development of Christian teenagers, but I also believe that part and parcel with good, effective counseling is pointing teenagers to their gifting and potential. We cannot just deal with the symptoms of dysfunction and fail to concentrate on defining and then prayerfully speaking proper function over the lives of our young people.

the future focus

By focusing on the future, we bring meaning to the present. By focusing on the future, we help teenagers realize that they can and will survive the pains of the present, even as they have already withstood the pressures of the past. For young people who are caught in a painful present, we must introduce them to the people they can be in the future if they resist the temptation to allow the past or the present to predict, or pre-speak, their future. **The prophetic coach does not just deal with the past, but also helps young people see their God-ordained and grace-empowered future.** This is the work of a true Samuel.

coaching tevin

Tevin Virtue was not yet a teenager when I met him. His older brother was dating one of the older teenagers in my youth church. As the dutiful girlfriend, she brought Tevin, her boyfriend's little brother, with her to one of our activity nights to play the crazy games we used to play on Friday nights with our junior high students.

Tevin was a thin boy with eyes that seemed almost too big for his head. He had long arms and legs that hung off his skinny torso like loose, half-hung appendages, promising that one day this little boy would stand tall over my head. His voice had yet to change, and so through his voice that was too high to match the gravity of his questions, I began to get to know Tevin.

> The prophetic coach does not just deal with the past, but also helps young people see their God-ordained and grace-empowered future.

Each night I would talk to him over the phone as he pelted me with questions too mature for his years. Questions about the nature and character of God and the meaning of divine justice. It was almost two years before he began to trust me enough to open up, and I began to understand the basis for these haunted questions.

Tevin had been raised in church to be religious, but his religious parents had some very serious problems. His father was an ugly and abusive drunkard who paid more attention to his drinking buddies than he did to his son, and Tevin was left both lonely and confused. He wondered how the loving and wonderful God they told him about at the expensive Christian school he attended could allow him to be fathered by a man who was so cruel, violent, and heartless. He wondered why his prayers for his father to change went unanswered and why God would play the cruel joke of having a church on every corner and yet being so remote from the pains of people.

To most of Tevin's questions I had no answers to give. I tried to help him see his father not in his addiction but through his addiction. I told him that people are not always what they do but are sometimes trapped in their actions. I prayed with Tevin that God would give him the strength and grace to forgive and release his father, and I assured him that the God of heaven had heard every single one of his prayers. I reminded Tevin that the fact that he had survived the violence and insanity in his home was an indication that God's grace had not abandoned him or his family.

> Sometimes the only key to the prison of your past is to fall in love with your future.

And then I challenged Tevin to be a better man than his father. I told him that because Tevin had a strong and real relationship with God, he would be able to overcome the temptations that had overcome his father. I told him that he would be an excellent father one day and an excellent husband. I told him that he would be a man of excellence and stature who would have a positive influence on the world and on his family.

I told Tevin that simply because his father had fallen into the trap of substance abuse did not mean he would have to be like his father. I pointed him not at the past or even at his present; instead, I challenged him to fall in love with his future.

Sometimes the only key to the prison of your past is to fall in love with your future.

Tevin fell in love with his future and is now completing his education at an elite university. He desires to serve the world as a youth pastor. If you sit with him today, he can overwhelm you with the things he has thought up to assist young people in broken homes and losing situations. He has not only fallen in love with his future, but he has fallen madly in love with the idea that he can help others to change their future as well.

I believe that Tevin will become an excellent youth pastor. From his own experience, he now knows how to light the way for students. Because he has found his own way out of the darkness of despair, I believe he will serve as a light of inspiration to his charges. I believe he will teach them how to find the grace to live in their present, even as he teaches them to focus on the grace that God has already extended to their future.

Only Jesus' light comes to give us illumination and to dispel the darkness. The light of salvation brings clarity to the situations in our lives. When that light is turned on in the lives of teenagers, they can see where they are going. When the light comes on, we can see where they have come from; and when the light comes on, we can see who they really are. They begin to see that they were winners all along.

Jesus' light gives teenagers the inspiration to face their present and the hope that they desperately need to keep on marching fearlessly into their future.

youth ministry **insights** ─────────────────────────

Here's a short list of biblical losers who became winners after powerful encounters with God's grace.

- Matthew
- Rahab
- Ruth
- Philip the Evangelist
- Nehemiah
- Jonah
- Moses
- Paul
- all of Jesus' disciples, except Judas
- the smart thief on the cross

As a prophetic coach, use these biblical examples to teach young people what can happen in their lives when they give into God's grace.

chapter 8

developing the negative

"But the Lord said to Samuel, 'Do not consider his appearance or his height, for I have rejected him. The Lord does not look at the things man looks at. Man looks at the outward appearance, but the Lord looks at the heart' " (1 Samuel 16:7).

Young people are like photographs. They must be properly illuminated to capture a clear image. They must be protected from outside influences, and they must be carefully and systematically developed before being displayed.

God was not deterred at all by how David appeared on the outside. God looked deep into the heart of the boy David and discerned that he would grow to be a man after his own heart (Acts 13:22). The negativity of David's family, or even the negativity of the perceptions of Samuel himself, did not hinder God's decision or deter his favor. God chose instead to develop the negative through life experiences into the image of a king.

And if the young David was a photograph, then certainly the prophet Samuel was the flash that God used to light up the subject. He came like a lightning bolt into David's life. Unexpected and unannounced, he pierced the darkened landscape of David's life and brought light.

unexpected and unannounced

David did not expect to be invited to the dinner with Samuel. The whole household had cleaned themselves up and prepared themselves to sit in the presence of this great and holy man, except for David. The invitation had not been heralded to the sheepfold, so while the rest of the household—and indeed the whole town—was in an uproar, David was not caught up in the hype and excitement because Samuel's coming seemed as if it would have no impact on his life.

Youth workers should not be surprised when the young people we seek to serve take weeks, months, or even years to accept that we really have come to give them godly guidance and assistance. We have to realize that many of these young people have never been invited to life's party and so are simply in a state of shock that we would actually seek to pull them to the side and speak into their lives.

We have to realize that our coming was not announced, that no John the Baptist preceded our coming or heralded our arrival. Many teenagers think (as David probably thought as Samuel anointed him), "Are you talking to me?" We cannot allow their coldness—which is often just a defense mechanism, an emotional wall they have erected to avoid being hurt again—to hinder us from continuing to express Christ's love and grace to them. They are just dazzled and dazed by the light of Christ's love, like deer caught in the headlights of an oncoming car. They are emotionally paralyzed by an encounter with their divine destiny.

In the same way, Samuel walked unannounced into David's life and, without fanfare or warning, changed everything. He anointed him not behind the barn or in the woods far from the prying and envious eyes of men. He anointed him in the presence of his older brothers, all of whom had been passed up for that particular position of favor.

a shock to the system

I am not blessed to have any biological brothers, so I do not know what it is to be at odds with an older brother. But I have seen brothers quarrel over many things: bicycles, video games, or even an old stick. I have seen them fight fiercely because someone gave one of them a toy that the other one wanted. Household wars have been waged over much less. But can you imagine the strife that would be stirred up if one brother were given a kingdom to rule while his seven older brothers were handed a younger brother as their future ruler?

One can only imagine how this news affected the family dynamics in Jesse's household. I imagine the memory of the anointing oil running out of Samuel's horn and down the face of David was indelibly engraved upon the synapses of his older brothers' minds. And based on the way David's older brother Eliab spoke to him before David encountered Goliath, we can infer that they treated him with disdain from that day forward:

"When Eliab, David's oldest brother, heard him speaking with the men, he burned with anger at him and asked, 'Why have you come down here? And with whom did you leave those few sheep in the desert? I know how conceited you are and how wicked your heart is; you came down only to watch the battle' " (1 Samuel 17:28).

Can you hear the teasing and put-downs his brothers probably rained down on David's head? This prophesy had not been anticipated by anyone in the family, and sometimes good news takes time to find good soil in the hearts of people.

This news was not only a shock to David; it had to be a shock to all his brothers. The system had been set upon its ears. The least was to be the greatest, and the last was to be the first.

God continued the pattern of choosing the last born to rule over the firstborn as he did with Jacob and Esau, Manasseh and Ephraim, Joseph and the sons of Israel. God chose to shock the system and switch the birth order. We can only imagine the kind of turmoil this switch caused within the system of Jesse's home, as it relates to David's relationship with his brothers.

Likewise, youth workers and counselors should work to help prepare the young people we are serving to be resisted, rebuffed, or rejected by the families or social systems they were embraced by before they came to know Christ. This is especially true when young people are coming out of losing environments. Often when teenagers start to attend church services or youth meetings, their families and social systems become agitated. This can be particularly disconcerting to the youth worker or minister when teenagers are coming out of toxic or even violent behavior. One would think family members and friends would be happy to see their loved ones make positive steps, but this is not always the case. Sometimes when one member of a family or social system steps into the glorious light of salvation, that light can cause others within the system to be agitated. Sometimes they fear that the teenager will leave them or will begin to believe he or she is too good for the others in the system. Or sometimes the others in the system are afraid that the young person will begin to view them negatively now that he or she is in the light and can see.

one mother's shock

Years ago I began to host a huge youth meeting on Good Friday every year. God's grace was with us, and each year hundreds of teenagers from across our region would walk down the aisle, many for the first time, and dedicate their lives to Christ. For weeks and weeks after the meeting, parents from across the region would call and write my youth church staff and praise God and thank us for sharing such an in-your-face message with their young people. But one day about two weeks after one of these meetings, I got a call from an agitated mother. Her daughter, who had made a profession of faith and had joined the youth church at a powerful Good Friday service, had really allowed God to turn her life around. The mother told me that her teenage daughter had broken off her relationship with her twenty-two-year-old boyfriend. The mother told me that her daughter was praying regularly and reading her Bible. The mother even told me that her daughter was working to be more obedient and being more helpful around the house.

By this time I was at a total loss as to why this mother was sounding so upset with me over the phone. I said, "Praise God, this all sounds great, so why do you sound so upset?"

She proceeded to tell me that since that Friday night her daughter had been reading the Bible. That very morning her daughter had sat calmly on the edge of her bed and in a spirit of meekness told her, "Mom, you are a fornicator!" Every weekend the mother would leave her oldest daughter in charge of her younger daughter so the mother could spend the weekend at her boyfriend's apartment. The mother, of course, had never taught her daughter that this kind of behavior was not normative to Christian people. Her mother would regularly attend Sunday services.

The mother was incensed and accused me of "teaching my daughter that I am a fornicator." I apologized and assured the mother that I had not taught her daughter that the mother was a fornicator. I explained to her that I had simply preached on the finished work of the Cross and God's amazing power to save people from their sins. I told her that I had not preached against fornication but I had preached for salvation. I told her that her daughter had begun to search the Scriptures so she could understand for herself what God required from his children.

I told that mother that I had not told her daughter that the mother was a fornicator, but then I asked her if she was. She hemmed and hawed a little and then admitted that she was. I asked her to please seek the counsel of the pastor of her home church so she could break the cycle of this habitual sin and be the kind of example her daughters so desperately needed.

I prayed with her, and although she had come on the phone roaring at me like a lion, she left that conversation in peace like a lamb, as the conviction of the Holy Spirit ministered to her life. I wish this story had a perfect and neat ending and that I could tell you that the mother allowed God to turn her life around. But like most of life, this story does not have a neat ending. After six months of allowing her daughter to attend and be active in our youth church, the mother decided to return to her relationship with her old boyfriend and totally forbade her daughter from coming to our youth church.

The daughter called me at my office and through tears told me of her mother's final decision. I quickly admonished her to adhere to her mother's decision and told her that she must totally honor her mother as the Bible had declared, even in this hard decision (Exodus 20:12). I told her that when she came of age and could make her own decision as to where she would worship, the church would still be there. I told her that her salvation was not built upon where she went to worship but upon who she chose to worship. I assured her that Jesus would give her the grace to live with her mother's decision. We prayed not just for her mother to change her mind, but also for Jesus to touch her mother's life.

I then referred her to the youth pastor at the church her mother regularly attended and let him know I was sending a promising teenage girl to his group.

This young lady was not the first young person whose family system had a negative reaction to God's higher call. And sadly, she was not the last. Over the years I have learned to prepare young people to roll with the emotional punches they can experience as friends and family members begin to see positive changes in their lives.

Sometimes when the rock of salvation falls unexpectedly into the puddle of our lives, it causes such righteous ripples that it displaces the waters and totally rearranges the relationships in our pool. These ripples can sometimes seem like shock waves to the friends and family members of young people who live in losing situations. So youth workers, parents, and counselors must be prepared to minister to the feelings of rejection and displacement that a rapid change in lifestyle can have on a young person who has made a decision for and a commitment to Christ.

the darkroom

My seven-year-old son loves to take pictures. To make funny faces and then to record them forever seems to tickle his fancy and quicken his puckish grin. When he was five years old, his maternal grandmother bought him a Polaroid camera so he wouldn't have to wait so long for the pictures to be developed. He simply had to point and then press, and like magic the images would appear upon the surface of those square white projectiles that emerged from his camera. The process was as instant as the gratification. But the development of young people who are emerging from negative and losing cycles is not often so quick or so tidy.

Indeed, in this age of Polaroid cameras and now the instant images from video and digital cameras, I think the old way of developing pictures is a better metaphor for how young people are developed into winners. In the days of old, the photographer would have to take the negative into a darkroom and go through a series of steps in order to produce a clear picture.

I think this metaphor better approximates the process of youth development that youth workers must master if they are to impact the lives of teenagers who seem like they are born to lose, even when we know that they are destined to win.

Even when they are still in the "darkroom," they are in the development process. The darkroom is an important part of the process. If the picture did not start as a negative and then go back into the darkroom, it would never emerge with clarity and brilliance.

Sometimes God allows young people to go back into the darkroom so he can develop the negative of their lives.

Sometimes they come to Christ but must return to negative homes and to negative schools and to negative neighborhoods, but God knows how to use those negative situations to form them into the image of his dear Son.

In fact, the youth worker or pastor can make a gross error in telling teenagers that their whole lives are going to turn around completely as they make a commitment to Christ Jesus. Most often, Christ calls them back into the darkroom so he can complete the process.

tell the truth

We preachers do a disservice to our listeners when we promise them a bed of roses and images of rose-colored tomorrows. Young people can be shocked to find out that their lives did not change overnight and that the situations that threaten them daily do not always instantly abate and sometimes grow even more tumultuous. We have to tell them the truth. We must tell them that when they come to Christ, God has begun a process of perfection in their lives. God and God alone knows when their outward situations will catch up to the divine peace that God speaks over our lives when we give our lives to him.

give them hope

We must tell them the truth but also give them hope. They can find hope in the reality that the development process has begun. They can find hope in knowing that the same God who found them in a world of darkness will not leave them locked up in the darkroom. They can find hope in the fact that the negative is always the exact opposite of what the picture will turn out to be and that God, who has begun good works in their lives, is always able and willing to complete the process.

That God places his princes in pastures before he places them in palaces should give our teenagers hope.

I think it is so very important to remember that David did not become the king of all Israel as soon as Samuel anointed him. David went back to the sheepfold still soaked in the oil of kings. This should give our teenagers hope. A young person can be destined for greatness, even while seeming to be trapped in a situation of despair. **That God places his princes in pastures before he places them in palaces should give our teenagers hope.** God taught David to sing, worship, and wage war while he was still with the sheep. And while you could not have detected an instant change in David's life, God had already begun to do a work in David's life that could not and would not be detected with a cursory inspection until the moment he was crowned the king.

The darkroom, then, is the place of development, and the negative is only an indication of the greatness God's grace will produce in the life of the teenager.

They tell me the photographer dips the picture into different chemical solutions in order to prepare the picture. In the same way, Samuel smeared and covered the boy David with the anointing oil as an outward sign to him and to us that God was dipping the negative of David's life into a solution that would develop him into a king.

trUE SUCCESS

Success is not a location; it is a destination. It is not just arriving at one point in life or climbing to some height of achievement. It is the constant process of going toward the point where God has told us to go. True success can be found only in the fulfillment of God's will for our lives. It is not an amount of money, nor is it a level of educational attainment. Success is not what people see; it is found in the fulfillment of what God has already spoken. In fact, even when young people are living in losing situations, if they are in God's developmental process, they already are winners.

After David had his encounter with Samuel, he returned to the sheep. Even though David had changed, his situation had not yet changed. He had received the spirit of a winner, and his first task in life was to win in that losing situation. He now had the winning spirit. A spirit is invisible, an intangible aspect of an individual. It is that quiet voice that says deep inside of a person, "Even though the situation looks bad, I am not a bad person. Even though the environment I am in is negative, I can still be positive. I can sing in a negative environment. I can work and worship even when I am surrounded by people who do not understand or appreciate who I am, or who I will become. Even in a losing environment, I can still be a winner."

Soaking wet with anointing oil, David went back to the sheep, and he returned to the menial tasks to which he had been assigned. He was in the same position to be developed for another one. Yes, David went back to being a keeper of the sheep, but the sheep would not keep him. He went back to the same situation, but even though the situation was the same, David was not.

David's brothers could see only a shepherd boy, not the winning spirit. All they could see was their little brother, who had been tasked to watch over a few sheep. But thanks be to God that his grace is not hindered by the perceptions of men, nor is it buttressed by the opinions of people. God chooses who he will, and he prefers the weak and the humble. Parents, youth workers, and all of us who are called to minister to young people who are living in losing systems and cycles must constantly remind our teenagers that whoever God calls a winner is going to win—even when the odds are against it. "If God is for us, who can be against us?" (Romans 8:31b).

Success is not a location; it is a destination.

Think about these questions. Consider discussing them with someone else on your youth ministry team.

* When have you been discouraged by the slow progress of change in a young person's life?

* How can you see more clearly the process of God working in the lives of the young people in your group?

* Which teenagers in your group are in the darkroom right now?

* How can you give those teenagers a vision for what God is doing in their lives?

* Who needs you to act as a flashbulb in his or her life, illuminating it with God's truth and calling?

chapter 9

making the change

"So Samuel took the horn of oil and anointed him in the presence of his brothers, and from that day on the Spirit of the Lord came upon David in power. Samuel then went to Ramah" (1 Samuel 16:13).

One of the benefits of growing older in ministry to young people is that as people see you successfully influencing young people by the power of God's grace, older people—too old to be members of the youth ministry—start to seek you out for counsel. Not for counsel on how to better serve young people, although equipping youth workers in this way is still one of the defining passions of my lifework, but for counsel on how to turn their adult lives around.

These days this kind of phone call is pretty common. Very often I receive phone calls or visits from adults who are looking for positive ways to improve their lives and productivity and who sense that my strange style of motivation can help them. But that's today. Ten years ago it was very unusual for adults to ask my advice on anything besides how to better reach and minister to their children.

To be perfectly honest, for many years I avoided having serious sessions with adults because I felt my straightforward style of confronting issues was too abrasive for people who had not experienced the tenderness of my pastoral ministry firsthand. I felt comfortable pushing hard on the kids I had spent hundreds of hours with or had helped get jobs or get out of jail. I felt like they would understand that I loved them and only wanted them to activate their potential. I was a little worried that "grown-ups" who had not heard me speak or participated in my programs would have a hard time with me saying, "Suck it up!" or "Get over it!"

Perhaps I have mellowed over the years, or maybe my pastor, Bishop T.D. Jakes, has had a great impact on how I view adults. He once told me that adults are "just grown-up teenagers, fraught with fears and failures and wrestling with the same issues that teenagers encounter, only at the next stage and age of development." And these words have stayed with me and enabled me to see my adult counselees with a clearer pastoral eye. Whatever the reason, now I meet with adults almost as much as I meet with teenagers. God has given me great success in motivating them to overcome their adult challenges.

But ten years ago, I had not yet met Bishop T.D. Jakes and had not felt the warmth of his pastoral heart or been modeled by the uniqueness of his God-given insight into the hearts of men and women. So back then I just avoided the "grown-ups" and referred them to pastors who specialized in adult ministry, no matter how hard or long they clamored for my attention. I just didn't want to hurt anybody's feelings.

One grown-up teenager

But one morning ten years ago, a grown man—a man some years older than I was—called my office seeking to meet with me. He veiled his true purpose for our meeting under another heading, something about ministry to young people, so we set a time and a place and agreed to meet for lunch.

I came to the little soup and salad place where we were slated to meet, thinking we would hash out some arrangement that would benefit the young people of the youth church. But just five minutes into the conversation, we had completely settled all the details, all of them completely favorable to my youth. I knew that if he was going to be this generous with his resources and contacts, he could have told me that over the phone and saved his valuable time for meeting with somebody more important than I was. I began to feel like there was another issue on his heart that he was dying to share with me. So I encouraged him to open up and tell me what was on his heart.

Through buttoned collar and power tie, this professional man began to show me the teenage boy that he kept carefully hidden underneath his professional demeanor. He began to tell me how he had made such a mess of his career, finances, and family and that he earnestly needed somebody who would tell him what he should do. He had been to others, and they had been too busy or too polite or too falsely encouraging to tell him what he was doing wrong. He said after a season of prayer, he felt that God had laid me squarely upon his heart as someone who could effectively mentor him to the next level of his own personal development.

My first reaction was to back away and refer him to a counselor who normally dealt with adults, but there was something in his question, a level of honesty and openness, that made me feel like I could really help him. I felt a compassion come over me, along with a clarity that comes when one can step back from the forest of another man's life and begin to see the trees.

This man was a winner. He had all the tools to win; what he lacked was the mindset to see himself as a winner. Underneath the Brooks Brothers ensemble and the wingtip shoes, I saw somebody who expected life to hand him a losing hand, so he had always just accepted anything out of life without critique, complaint, or challenge. To the casual observer, he was a winner, but in his mind's eye, he was a loser. He had allowed the negative words of people to so influence his personal perception that even when he won in life, he still felt like he was a loser.

I knew I could help him. I pulled a ballpoint pen from my jacket pocket and began to take notes on a napkin. I mapped out his childhood, his family system, his career choices, and his educational decisions. I had him tell me about his marriage and the dynamics he was facing at home, and then I asked him a question that I ask almost everyone I counsel, lead, or mentor. "Mr. Winters," I said, "What do you want?" The question almost knocked him out of his seat, like somebody had hit him over the head with a Louisville Slugger. No one had ever asked him what he wanted, nor had he ever had the guts to ask himself that question. All he knew was that he was totally unsatisfied with how his life was turning out. Even though he was a strong Christian man, possessing an earnest faith in Christ, he had given little or no conscious thought to what he wanted out of life.

"I don't know." he said.

"Yes, you do, sir. You are just too cowardly to speak it out of your mouth because then you know you will be responsible to shoot for what you have said."

The forcefulness of my response was again like another slug to his head. If I had had any sense at all, I would have been nervous that he was going to grab me from across the table and anoint me with a bowl of clam chowder, but I was too far into him by then to be thinking about me.

"Spit it out, man!" I said evenly. "You have been waiting your whole life to articulate what you want out of this life without being judged; now it's your turn. Don't blow it."

I remember how he leveled his brown eyes at me, and like he was reading off some invisible teleprompter, he began to tell me his life dreams while I finished off my salad. What was so shocking was how wonderful and well thought out his life plan was. It was not overly complicated, nor was it ornately ambitious. It was a very good plan, and I told him it was.

"Mr. Winters, that is so easy," I said with all the certainty I could communicate to him with words, facial expression, and tone. I then turned my napkin around and showed him that in each phase of his life plan, he already had the talent base or personal asset he needed to complete the task. I showed him on paper how he already had what he needed to reach his goals. I told him that if I had what he already had, I would be ruling the known universe, and "God knows," I said with a big smile, "I am no smarter or more talented than you are. I just believe I can do whatever God gives me to do."

"Mr. Winters, all we really need to work on is your ability to see yourself through God's eyes. If you ever realize that God has already given you the grace and the talent base to accomplish these tasks, there is no end to what you can accomplish."

For the next six months, I regularly met with Mr. Winters. I had numerous conversations with him and his wife, and I watched how God's grace began to empower first him and then his entire household to accomplish their dreams. Three years after our first meeting, he had accomplished all the goals he had shared with me, many of which he had spent half his life trying to achieve, and he was beginning to formulate more. What had changed was not his talents or the assets at his disposal. What had changed was his ability to appropriate the grace of God to reach into the details of his personal life and personal perception.

the importance of self-perception

God's grace doesn't just raise our self-esteem. God changes our mind-set and our self-perception. Mr. Winters received a winning spirit, and that spirit affected his wife, empowered his children, and changed their lives. He made the change. He recognized God's grace in his life and was empowered by that grace to change his mind and then his attitude, and then he changed his future.

Right now, all around you are people who are losing. And the only reason they are losing is that they have been told they are going to lose. Either other people or they themselves have told them they are going to lose. Even though they may be excellent Christians, they still believe they are going to lose.

When teenagers come from environments that constantly reinforce to them that they're going to lose, very often they will live to fulfill this self-perception. They will gravitate toward negative actions, people, and habits because they believe they're going to fail. Sometimes they will even pursue lives of crime because they believe they can't make it or achieve in the legitimate world. Amazingly, even if they find great "success" in lives of crime, they will not extrapolate from those dark achievements a belief that they can compete in the legitimate arena, because they still think of themselves as losers.

They see themselves as losers and earnestly do not believe they can make it in life on the up-and-up.

Because a life of drug-dealing or gangbanging or street crime seems to be so much easier than legitimate labor, they will risk death, disfigurement, and imprisonment rather than join the rank and file of us normal working stiffs. Why? Because **they see themselves as losers and earnestly do not believe they can make it in life on the up-and-up.**

But this tragic phenomenon, this losing way of thinking, is not limited to the haunted gutters of the ghetto; it reaches all the way to the quiet bedroom communities of America's suburbs. How many talented people dream of starting businesses, building inventions, writing books, or attending universities but because they are too afraid they might lose, grab firmly on to the horns of the altar of status quo and beg God for mercy instead of appropriating God's grace? How many great minds chose low-ball classes or switched majors and, therefore, forfeited their dream careers simply to be successful in the mirage of mediocrity?

How many teenagers never tried out for the school play, never went to audition for the band, or never tried out for the team? How many teenagers never tried to reach out and make friends? How many sat in utter confusion in the back of the class rather than raise their hands and ask simple questions of the teachers who may have sacrificed financially to be sitting in that class with them?

These teenagers think they're losers, so they lose. We who are called to minister to them must help them to make the change—the change in their thought processes to help them believe in God, and to believe in the God who is active in their own lives.

bee somebody

Solomon tells us to look at the ant and to learn from its habits (Proverbs 6:6), but I am constantly encouraged by the bumblebee. He comes flying into my mind because even though he does not appear on paper to be aerodynamic, he still is able to fly. The bumblebee reminds me of the many young people I pastored and mentored who did not look like they could fly when I met them, but today, like bumblebees, they are flying in life.

In the 1930s an aerodynamicist sat down and quickly attempted to mathematically work out on paper just how the bumblebee was able to fly. Using coarse and simple math equations, he could not work out how a bumblebee was able to fly. The aerodynamicist could not factor in all the details and was not able to capture the power and ingenuity of the bee.

I can understand why someone would question how a bee is able to fly, laden as bees are with their purpose of spreading pollen and making honey. They are so laden with purpose that just looking at them, a person might feel sure that a bumblebee would never get off the ground. In fact, if you take a moment to observe a bumblebee, you will see that he does not move like the butterfly, and the fly is smaller and more aerodynamic and seems to be able cut through the air.

The bumblebee comes lumbering to my mind, like a flying semitrailer working tenaciously at the assignment God has given him. He goes from flower to flower on wings that look like they are unable to sustain the weight of this busy bug. And yet this insect is able to fly and has been flying since time turned on the light for the simple reason that no one has been able to communicate to the bumblebee and tell him that he doesn't look like he should be able to fly.

They can fly not on the almost transparent wings of the bumblebee, but on the totally invisible wings of God's grace.

We must teach our teenagers that even though their life situations might try to make them feel as if they are too heavy to fly, they have been built to fulfill a divine purpose. As long as they key into their divine assignments, they can fly. It doesn't matter that they do not look like anyone else or that they do not come from the right family or pedigree. If God calls them to fly, they can fly. Even if the scientists and statisticians of this century do not have an equation that can tell them how they are flying, and even if it doesn't seem to work out on paper, they can fly over abuse, fly over abandonment, fly over poverty, and fly over pain. **They can fly not on the almost transparent wings of the bumblebee, but on the totally invisible wings of God's grace.**

too heavy not to fly

It is not that teenagers are too heavy to fly. The truth is that they are too heavy with their divine purpose not to fly. There are many people who really are able to fly but have been told they cannot and are so transfixed and so attracted by their situation that they are distracted from success.

When young people are told forcefully and repeatedly that the Word of God declares they are winners (1 John 5:4), and when God's Word begins to tear down the barriers of their poor self-perception and establish a firm foundation of faith in God's ability to make real his will in their lives, they begin to believe they can be somebody. They begin to believe that they can win despite the odds, not because they're not losers but because they're teaming up with God, and God is always a winner.

The Bible tells us that after David was anointed by Samuel, the Spirit of the Lord came upon him. It tells us that the touch of the Holy Spirit flowed over him and through him inwardly as the oil flowed over him outwardly. David was changed. He was no longer solely a shepherd boy. Now he was a shepherd boy who had the Spirit of the Lord upon his life. Even though he was still a shepherd boy, he had been touched by the divine. His destiny had been set, and his whole life was changed. He had the winning spirit. His life had not been outwardly changed, but his spirit had been touched by the power, presence, and unlikely favor of God. David might have looked like a loser to his brothers, but he was now a winner. He might have appeared like one who would never fly over his circumstances, the circle of situations that surrounded his life and destiny, but now he had the power to become great. Now he had the calling to be great, and all he needed to do was prepare his heart, his hand, and his mind-set for the great day when he would become the king God had called him to be.

What a mind-blowing miracle this had to be to David! He was changed by the power of God. He had the winning Spirit of God on his life, and he would never again be the same.

the touch of the divine

Teenagers do not always initially view themselves as victorious and able to overcome all the obstacles they may face in life. But when they get a glimpse into the glory of God, his power and majesty, this new view of God begins to unlock their ability to believe that, even though the odds are stacked against them, this great God of power and majesty is able to save them from their situations.

The prophet Isaiah tells us that he saw the Lord (Isaiah 6:1). God revealed himself to Isaiah in a powerful vision. Isaiah could not be defined as a prophet until God had been defined in his life as the king. The Lord revealed himself as the greatest king Isaiah would ever know or see—a king who was high and lifted up with a train of glory that filled the temple; a king who could not be corrupted by time, sin, or death; a king who was holy. This is how God introduced himself to Isaiah.

God introduced himself to Moses in the form of a bush, and to Paul he came as a blinding light on the road to Damascus, but he came to the prophet Isaiah as a king. God demonstrated to him that he alone is the King Eternal and the Lord of both the living and the dead. Once Isaiah prioritized God correctly and realized that God was higher than any earthly king, God positioned him on the divine life path that God had intended for Isaiah before time had begun.

When the Word of God cuts through all the distractions and outside stimuli that hinder young people who are caught in losing situations and finds a resting place in the hearts, minds, and spirits of those young people, then you will start to see them redefine how they see themselves.

"If this great God cared enough to die for me, I must have value," they begin to say. The cross of Christ gives all of us our value, and so we Christians don't just have self-esteem. We have been esteemed by God, through the sacrifice of Christ Jesus. As parents, youth workers, and counselors begin to walk teenagers through the wonderful work of salvation, even if the teenagers are still overwhelmed by their situations, they will begin to see that God cares about them despite the situations they find themselves in. This is the touch of the divine, and this vital step is the genesis of a changed life and a regenerated mind-set.

God's Word reaches down through the muck and mire of our everyday existence and touches our hearts. His Word redefines who we are. It shakes us out of the negativity and breaks us out of the cycle of loss that attempts to grip and stifle our spiritual, emotional, and social growth and development.

The touch of the divine makes a difference even when teenagers are still looking at their situations and don't recognize and realize that they are *still standing* in their situations. Even if they are still so caught up in what they are *going through* that they have yet to realize they have been going through what they are going through, the touch of the divine will still give them the self-esteem and self-value they need so desperately to begin to change their mind-set. They will begin to see that even if they don't yet believe they are winners, over two thousand years ago, a winner bled and died for them so they could win.

The touch of the divine is the first step to helping young people make the change to a mind-set of someone with a winning spirit.

the sound of applause

The second step to helping teenagers change their mind-set and receive a winning spirit is creating a powerful and positive environment in which teenagers can be celebrated and applauded just for overcoming the everyday obstacles they face.

Remember that Samuel did not anoint David away from the eyes and notice of other people. Samuel poured that precious oil on David's head in his own environment and in front of people who knew who David was and where he had just come from. People who had known him all his life stood and watched him be anointed as a king. This is vital because perhaps this was the first time David had been given public notice and acclaim as someone important, not only to his family but to the whole nation. Perhaps the people who watched David be anointed did not clap and applaud as the oil flowed down his ruddy face, but certainly the looks of shock and amazement emblazoned across their faces were more than enough to make him feel like this was a special day in his life.

As I work with inner city youth, I am confronted constantly by teenagers who look at the situations they have been raised in and are overcome by the odds against them.

They look at the projects and the housing developments and the onslaught of crime and the war of drugs and the destruction of the welfare state and reformation of social care systems. In the face of all these negative factors and the effect they have on teenagers' lives, I have seen young people silently and sadly write themselves off. Too often, they look at their situations without fully comprehending that they have still survived the situations. Yes, they have problems, but as long as they have life, the problems do not have them. They are living in their situations.

Many times I have, both through one-on-one counseling and preaching, applauded these teenagers who have just survived this hard life. I love to anoint them with the positive power of God's Word while they are living in their tough environments and while they are in front of their families and friends. I love to applaud them for surviving the trouble and applaud them in the midst of the pain. I applaud them for being winners by the grace of God.

They cope with losing situations every day. I tell them over and over that they already are winners. They may not be in winning situations, but they're winners because they are able to survive day after day, night after night; they are able to get up every day; they are able to not just lose their minds, although they live under pressures that people from other communities could not stand one day. They are winners who must be celebrated, saluted, and applauded. I applaud them, and I applaud the God who has so graced and empowered them to live and move and to become the people God wants them to be.

These young people who are living in losing systems really are winners. When youth workers or even parents who live with them begin to sit down with their teenagers and agree that the odds have been stacked against them but consistently highlight the success teenagers are emerging into, those teenagers start to have some eureka moments and to realize that they're winners—they really are winners.

I have often stood up and physically applauded young people for simply surviving their neighborhoods. I scream and shout and clap my hands because God has kept them alive. I have slapped many a young man on the back or hugged a young lady about the neck and said, "You go, boy!" or "You go, girl!" just because they have not gone crazy in the midst of insane situations.

I have taken this a step further and created a laundry list of programs and a plethora of pageants that allow the church and the secular community to help me applaud young people. They are taking small steps, but these small steps will change their tomorrows. It may be for Scripture memorization or singing a gospel song; it may be for learning a dramatic recitation or passing a simple Bible quiz. For all of these things, we applaud them.

Our young people need to hear us cheer. They need to hear us clap and say wonderful things about their work, their lives, and their future. In this way they get value not only from the Scriptures, but also from the positive affirmation of the church community at large and from their youth workers individually. Youth workers should not discount the value of their affirming and celebrating their teens, particularly when our teenagers are facing losing situations and toxic circumstances.

a taste of success

If you visit our youth church at the Potter's House on any night of the week, you will see young people who are very active. Our senior pastor, Bishop T. D. Jakes, has empowered me to build and structure a youth ministry that provides young people with "a place to go, something to do, and someone who cares." To carry out Bishop Jakes' vision for the youth God has entrusted him to impact, he has charged my staff and me to light a fire under our young people. When you come you will see young people in tutoring sessions; artistic instruction in drama or music; dance classes for jazz, break dancing, or hip-hop; and Bible classes that work to ground them in the Word.

We want our young people to be active and successful in ministry. The young people in the ministry might not have experienced success in any other aspect of their lives, but we have determined that through practice, preparation, and biblical training, our teenagers will be successful at the Potter's House.

At every youth service, young people are given an opportunity to demonstrate and showcase their talents before the youth congregation. Periodically, they stand before the entire church, with its thirty thousand-plus members, and praise and worship God through the artistic talents with which God has endowed them.

On more than one occasion, Bishop T.D. Jakes has allowed our teenagers to participate in his massively attended international conference and to serve and bless tens of thousands of people through their creative ministries.

At the Potter's House, we are always thrilled to see the congregants and conference delegates blessed by our youth ministry, but I am always equally as blessed to see the feeling of accomplishment and glow of success come over our young people as they stand on that great stage and worship the Lord.

You cannot image the joy our teenagers experience when their senior pastor or their pastor's wife stands and applauds all their hard work and preparation. It is as if someone turned a light on in their spirits, and I can almost see the flame of the winning spirit being fanned by the wind of their success.

Now don't get me wrong. We don't applaud these achievements because we want to give them a fake or phony affirmation. No, they work extremely hard to both learn and professionally present their talents. And when those teenagers walk away from that experience, they walk away knowing that they have worked hard and have been successful in blessing the people of God through their talents, skills, and gifts.

As a pastoral staff and as a church community, we have decided to concert our efforts to give our young people a taste of success. This is the third step in helping young people make the change in mind-set that enables them to embrace the winning spirit.

David did not face Goliath until after he had first experienced the success of being anointed instead of and in front of his brothers. That was his first taste of success. The first moment when he experienced the limelight on his face as that fragrant oil fell on his face. This was a glorious experience in the life of David, and I believe it was the defining moment of his life. But even this experience was not enough to prepare him to overcome the great champion of the Philistines. David had to first overcome a lion that attempted to take one of his sheep from the sheepfold. David took off right after that lion with nothing more than a shepherd's rod, a rock, and a sling, and he killed that lion. That was another taste of success.

The taste of success prepares and trains the pallet of our spirit to grow used to the taste of success. Like the first sweet taste of sugar in the mouth of a baby, this taste is instantly desirable. Over time, we will do the work required to receive this taste over and over again.

My first cousin, Kashleigh, was raised as a strict vegetarian, without meat, poultry, or refined sugar. She had never tasted white sugar or sugared cereals until she was seven years old. Even when she would spend the night over at our house, her mother would dutifully send a special unsweetened cereal over to our house with her so she wouldn't grow accustomed to the taste of white sugar. At the beginning of her life, she thought honey was the sweetest thing on the planet. Her mother's plan was working great until one day my cousin forgot to bring her cereal over with her and was forced to have a bowl of my Frosted Flakes, well-fortified with all that "yucky" sugar. Her little eyes became electrified as her mouth exploded with the flavor of the sugar, and she was instantly changed into sugar's number one fan. After seven years of being told that sugar was "yucky," all that careful and deliberate programming was erased by just one taste.

Likewise the taste of success can begin to systematically reprogram young people who have grown accustomed to losing. The taste of success builds faith, crystallizes confidence, and activates expectation. It can very rapidly develop a pallet for brighter days. The taste for success helps energize young people to push beyond the problems and obstacles that surround them and helps them believe they can achieve.

After David killed that lion, he discovered that he had the confidence to also confront a bear that attempted to take a sheep out of David's care. David gave chase to the bear and returned with the sheep carefully draped over his shoulders, leaving the mangy carcass of the bear strewn lifeless on the ground.

His chases after a lion and a bear demonstrate that David believed he would be successful. He had a winning spirit. When a lion comes to steal one of the lambs and then a bear comes to kill one of the lambs, David forsakes his own needs and fears and chases after these dangerous beasts. This level of boldness exemplifies the winning spirit.

My wife and I have a dog named Lady, and we love her dearly. She is a black and gray purebred bouvier des Flandres, who came with both pedigree and papers. She is a wonderfully bright dog that one of our parishioners gave to my son some years ago. Lady is not just our pet, she is family. We love Lady. We spend a great deal of our lives together in the back yard, walking Lady, brushing Lady, washing Lady. We love Lady. But as much as I love Lady, if a lion came into my back yard and snatched my prized and pedigreed bouvier des Flandres, I would not chase after the lion, certainly not armed only with a slingshot and a rock.

I would have to be perfectly honest with you and tell you that as much as I love my dog, we would have to let Lady go into her sweet reward before we would wrestle a lion or a bear so that she would be free. Loving Lady, I would go and bury her properly in a Christian fashion, hoping to see her on the other side of that crystal shore. I would not fight a bear for my dog.

Here is David fighting a lion and a bear that he might liberate and save his sheep. If this doesn't demonstrate the winning spirit, I don't know what does.

Later when David gave King Saul his verbal résumé for why he would be able to kill Goliath, he did not tell him about the kingly anointing he had received from Samuel. He related to King Saul how he had successfully overcome these two ferocious beasts. David told Saul of his taste of success.

Youth workers have to work to either highlight or sometimes even create real challenges and situations so their young people, those who really believe they are losers, can discover their winning potential by actually winning. Whether we do so through the arts or through sports or through educational challenges or simply by helping them see the little successes they are experiencing daily in life, we have to give them some of that "yucky" sugar until they have acquired a taste for it and developed the drive to go after it.

I believe it was an ancient Greek poet and philosopher who said, "The soul is dyed with the color of its thoughts." Youth leaders can help recolor their teenagers' thoughts and self-perceptions by helping them taste success. This third and potent key will help young people change their mind-set, reset the paradigm, and catch hold of a winning spirit.

youth ministry insights

Discuss these questions with your youth ministry team. It's a great idea to build an entire team meeting or even a retreat around these questions.

* In what ways are you helping teenagers in your group experience the touch of the divine?

- In what ways can you more effectively help them experience the touch of the divine?

- In what ways are you helping teenagers in your group experience the sound of applause?

- In what ways can you more effectively help them experience the sound of applause?

- In what ways are you helping teenagers in your group experience a taste of success?

- In what ways can you more effectively help them experience a taste of success?

chapter 10

off with his head

"So David triumphed over the Philistine with a sling and a stone; without a sword in his hand he struck down the Philistine and killed him. David ran and stood over him. He took hold of the Philistine's sword and drew it from the scabbard. After he killed him, he cut off his head with the sword" (1 Samuel 17:50-51a).

the main event

David's battle with Goliath marks the end of the first phase of David's life and the beginning of his meteoric rise to prominence and later royalty. This battle is the main event of his life. All the other problems and situations he faced were simply undercards in the boxing match of his life, and now he would fight the real heavyweight, Goliath.

He already had overcome his brothers with all of their negative words, thoughts, and actions. He had received the anointing of Samuel and held on to belief in God's plans for him, even though his fortunes had not been instantly altered and his function within the family had not changed. He had weathered the bleak blizzard of boredom in daily tending his father's sheep while he knew he was destined for the excitement of the palace. He had successfully defeated both the lion and the bear that had tried to steal his sheep out of the sheepfold. And now he was ready for Goliath.

Old Goliath believed he was looking at a boy carrying a shepherd sling, but he was looking at a boy who was carried by a winning spirit.

All these situations had served as excellent teachers to David, and he was ready for graduation day. With reckless abandon, David ran out after Goliath. The giant had no idea whom he was dealing with. **Old Goliath believed he was looking at a boy carrying a shepherd sling, but he was looking at a boy who was carried by a winning spirit.**

the indomitable winning spirit

David had gone through too much and waited too long for that opportunity to lose the battle. David knew too much about God and how his grace favors the weak to allow the negative thoughts, attitudes, and opinions of others to influence his decision. David had a winning spirit, and he was ready for the main event.

The winning spirit is too strong to be influenced by peer pressure. Once it has taken root in the life of a teenager, no peer can speak louder than its call to greatness.

No gang can beat it out. No girlfriend or boyfriend can coerce it to permanently surrender. The winning spirit is almost fueled by the words "you won't" and "you can't." These pernicious prognostications become the fertilizer that enriches the soil of hope, the wind that stokes the embers of belief into the hot flame of faith. When the winning spirit takes hold of a young person's imagination, it changes the person's paradigm and invades his or her personal mind-set of negative peer pressure to become positive. And even the hurtful words of loved ones will cause them to redouble their efforts just to silence the voices of their detractors and to prove to them that they can win.

This winning spirit was so strong in the life of David that even the king couldn't talk David out of his convictions. King Saul was an experienced soldier, but not even he had decided to take on Goliath. He tried to use his position of authority and experience to dowse the red-hot flame of David's desire, but not even the king, in all his courtly power, could command more respect than the winning spirit.

The high-minded people who drop negative words of doom and gloom upon the heads of young people cannot stop a young person who has caught this spirit. Their poisonous apples may fall from the loftiest branch of the tree of society. But instead of a headache, the teenagers—like Newton—get a fresh idea. This idea helps them understand their world better and then helps them rewrite the laws of their personal universe. Once teenagers have grabbed ahold of the winning spirit, every experience becomes an eureka moment and every problem, though painful, becomes an opportunity to win.

They start to show up for life every day. They punch the time clocks of their purpose and decide that each day they will give themselves 100 percent to the tasks and challenges they face because they now see each problem as an opportunity for them to rejoice in the grace of God.

I am not saying they become reckless but that they are no longer afraid to try or to fully commit themselves to a task. They leave nothing in the locker room, and they determine to discover what they could accomplish if they really tried.

confronting goliath

A few months ago a youth pastor friend of mine, whom I have known since he himself was a teenager, called me in the middle of the day. It was a rainy Saturday afternoon, so my little family was huddled around a roaring wood fireplace, watching a kids' movie on the television. It was raining outside, but because he sounded so confused I grabbed my hat, switched to the cordless phone, and decided to walk my dog, Lady, while we talked on the phone.

As I walked around in lazy circles in the back yard, getting wet, the youth pastor began to open his heart to me and told me why he was at his wit's end. He was in a money mess, a ministry conundrum, and a parental crisis.

He told me his job just wasn't paying him enough money to make the ends meet in his household. He went on to tell me in detail how he had approached his senior pastor about the problem, and now it seemed to him as if the senior pastor was refusing to meet with him to discuss the money problem or even any other ministry matters because things had gotten so heated in their last meeting.

He told me he had been trying to get on his pastor's schedule for months to no avail, and now the administrators at his church had just informed him that they were going to suspend his health benefits because of a financial crisis at the church. This was a great problem because his daughter had taken ill and was in need of an expensive medical procedure, and now they had no medical insurance to help cover the expense.

My friend is an awesome preacher who has a great testimony about how God rescued him out of the grip of drug abuse, gang activity, and crime, but he felt so powerless to do anything to defeat these problems.

He asked me what I thought he should do.

Now, half soaked to the bone, I asked him one of my favorite questions: "What would you do if money were no object and you had no fear?"

When he told me his answer, I told him I believed that was exactly what he should do. I told him he should apply himself to this challenge with the same ferocity he had exhibited to overcome his drug addiction in the past and that he should trust God to empower him to win over this ugly Goliath.

I reminded him that God is not broke, even when we are. I reminded this preacher of the gospel that the Bible teaches us that God is the alpha and the omega, the beginning and the end, and that is why God knows how to "make the ends meet." He has both ends covered.

I told him that God had not given him the spirit of fear but had empowered him through grace to lovingly lead his family in peace (2 Timothy 1:7).

I told him that he was a winner who had vanquished a giant stronger than this one and that I believed without question that he could overcome this problem.

After praying, we got off the phone. My friend was already coming up with solutions to his problem. My pastor, T.D. Jakes, has often told me, **"Prayer doesn't always change the situation; sometimes it changes you!"** This certainly was the case with my friend that rainy afternoon. He dried his eyes, and I put on some dry clothes, and God empowered him to change his situation.

One month later my friend called me back to let me know how things were working out for him and his family. It was late on a Thursday evening, and my wife, my young son, and I were sitting in our family room watching yet another kids' movie.

When I realized it was he on the phone, I instantly grabbed the dog's leash and my hat, thanked God it was not raining, and headed for the back yard.

He told me they had reset their budget to live within their means. He had reconciled with his pastor and had opted to take another position where the church had a strong benefit package. His daughter was flourishing with the medical treatments. He told me with pride that God had brought order to his household by first bringing order to his soul. He had the winning spirit.

"Prayer doesn't always change the situation; sometimes it changes you!"

confidence in god

We who are charged to teach young people how to win in life have to be reminded ourselves of the winner who lives within us. It is not that we have confidence in ourselves, but we have full confidence in the greater one who lives within us. When God shows up in our situation, he always demonstrates his power, first to change us in the midst of the problem and then to empower us to discover how to overcome the problem. Sometimes the greater revelation is not for us to see God show himself strong enough to change the situation. Sometimes it is for us to look beyond the problem and allow God to show us himself in the situation.

get in

Two-thirds of the word *win* is *in*. Unfortunately, most people will never win because they have locked themselves out of the arena of success. You have to be "in it" to win it.

Too often teenagers suffer from a lack of success because they are not really in it. They don't fill out the applications, they don't go for the interviews, they don't even attempt to study with all their might to prepare for the exams. Their mind-set is locked up in a losing attitude and losing spirit, and, therefore, they don't expend themselves to the point of success. In order to win, they have to be in. They have to get to the place where they don't care what they look like and they don't care what other people think about them. They have to be so convinced that if they put all of themselves into being successful, they will be.

Our educational system is failing because we are not challenging people to be all the way in. We give people minimal skills tests and train them to those tests and thus teach them minimal skills instead of teaching them to maximize their potential.

Sadly, even our churches are failing because we are not challenging people to be all the way in. Those of us in ministry should not encourage others to be laypersons; God doesn't need anyone lying around. We should encourage them to be "fray people": people who are willing to leap into the fray of ministry and fight for the goals and vision of the church. We need church members who are active and involved and empowered by the grace of God to fight the good fight of faith and to serve the community in a spirit of meekness, not weakness.

When people get into something and get lost in it, they are lost in their purpose. They are swimming in the ministry. They are like the prophet of old (Ezekiel 47:5). They have left the shoreline of their commitment to the work of the church, not to splash in the shallows but to launch out into the depths of the purpose of the church. No great swimmer ever swam without getting in the water, and no great Christian, young or old, ever made an eternal effect on the world without getting fully immersed in the deep and fast-moving waters of ministry.

When teenagers become empowered with a winning spirit and are plugged into the ministry of their local church, they become so jointed and joined to the vision and purpose God has for their own lives that they are too busy to be depressed. Parents and youth workers begin to see them excel to another level.

lions and giants and bears, thank god!

When David had returned to the sheepfold after Samuel's anointing, nothing had changed in his life but David. He went back with the new spirit of a winner upon him and adopted a whole new attitude toward sheep. He did not see the situation as a negative; he began to see the situation as a positive. David fell madly in love with the sheep and would take on all kinds of dangers and risks in order to be an excellent steward of his charges. In Psalm 23, David demonstrated how he had elevated his position in his mind. He boldly and metaphorically paralleled his role as a shepherd boy to that of the almighty God. Now that's the winning spirit!

Even when the oil had dried and washed away, that same winning spirit lingered on in David. David confronted Goliath, just as he had confronted the wild beasts that were threatening his sheep. He used the same spirit and the same methods to overcome the great champion of Gath that he had used to beat back the bear of the brush.

So the lion became a great opportunity to warm up for the bear, the bear became the warm-up for the giant, and the giant was the setup for the kingdom. I am sure that by the time David was cutting off Goliath's head, he was thanking God that the lion, the bear, and the giant had come into his life.

Just as Joseph viewed the day his brothers sold him into the bonds of slavery as a positive day in his life (Genesis 50:20), so it is with teenagers who have a winning spirit. What others would perceive as negatives in their lives, these teenagers start to view as very painful positives. When teenagers see the circumstances that should have destroyed them as the very things God is using to make them into champions, they are catching the winning spirit.

the defining moment

Whenever God wants to make a champion, he gives him or her a problem. The virgin Mary was pregnant before she was married—that's a problem. Moses had to liberate a people without an army to help him—that's a problem. Esther had to break all protocol and risk death to save her people. Paul had to win and work with the same people he had persecuted. Those are real problems. We are defined more by our problems then by anything else. Our faith is fired in the furnace of affliction and crystallized in the crucible of conflict.

The first thing God gave to his son Adam, the father of us all, was a problem. He charged him to keep up and after, with all his human limitations, a garden that God had made with his own spiritual force.

God gave him a job, a big job. How do you compete with God's gardening? How can any groundskeeper keep up with the dude who made the ground? God gave Adam a problem—he employed him in the family business. And through this problem God defined Adam as a person of dominion, purpose, and power. He gave him a problem to solve, and his identity came out at the end of the equation.

All over this nation, young men and women in the urban, suburban, and rural centers of America do not have positive relationships with their natural fathers. A whole generation of young men and women are not being defined by their parents and feel like they are being raised to lose in life.

You can tell when the winning spirit starts to grip the hearts of these young people because instead of seeing themselves as victims, they begin to view themselves as victors. Even if no one ever defined them as good, they realize they were good enough to survive their problems, and they know they are winners. They might have never received positive feedback, and two very critical or disinterested parents might have raised them, but they still made it. They defied the odds and made it to the other side of that lonely desert without the sweet water of positive affirmation. They made it, and that proves they are winners.

Their problems have defined them, and the eureka moment for them will be when they realize that God's grace has empowered them to survive. The true joy of my life as a minister and a motivator is in reminding people that they are still alive and, therefore, have all the power, purpose, and passion to both discover and fulfill the divine mandates on their lives.

Besides the day of salvation, the two most important dates in the lifetime of any person are not the birthing day and the dying day. They are not the wedding day or the day of first communion or joining a local church. **In my mind, besides the day of salvation, the most important day is the day we realize we have survived all the pain we have walked through because God's grace has kept us alive. The second most important day is the day we know why God kept us alive.**

breaking the walls

When I sit with young women and men for whom I am praying that God will give a winning spirit, I start the process by telling them just how incredible I think they are. I tell them they are incredible even though they might not see themselves that way. They might not have a positive self-image, and many of them are lacking a positive maternal or paternal voice in their lives. They might even be without strong family or community support systems or without complete and careful education; I call them great men and women of God and of excellence, just the same.

They might not look like it, but I call them great. Because despite the fact that they don't have what they should and they haven't been living in a way I can approve of or condone, I firmly believe that locked up behind those losing ways are winners screaming to get out. I know that God has already given them the potential to be great.

I believe that my words have the power to give life and to begin to erase all the negative words that might have filled their ears and hearts for years. I believe that positive words can begin to dismantle walls of negativity, pain, and disappointment. Positive affirmation has restorative power and becomes one of the lifelines that we can throw a young person who is caught in an undertow of loss.

Teenagers in losing situations have heard so many negative and hurtful words that in some communities they play competitions to see who can conjure the most painful insult. Most teenagers are so injured by the words of adults and their peers because they have never been taught to consider the thought processes and pain of the people who have said these words. Because they do not consider the sources of the negative words spoken over their destiny, they readily accept them as facts instead of seeing them as bitter grapes from an unkempt vine.

Jesus taught us that a bitter tree produces bitter fruit, and we must teach teenagers to reject the bitter words that come from the lips of bitter people. We must teach them not to fulfill those false prophesies, accepting them wholesale without examining closely who said them and why. Negative words hurt and cause young people to build emotional walls to protect themselves. Later, those protective walls become prison walls that hold them into a certain mode of behavior and become the structure of their self-image.

Every parent, teacher, youth worker, and pastor must be reminded repeatedly that each and every word has power—even an idle word. The Bible declares emphatically and without reservation that life and death are firmly fixed in the power of the tongue (Proverbs 18:21). Life and death are not in the tongue but in the power of the tongue.

The tongue is not just a muscle that moves in and about our mouths, producing sounds. The tongue has the power to plant something into the spirit of a young person to whom you are speaking. Words, both negative and positive, have the potential to take root and grow up in the life of the young person. This is critical to people who are dealing with young people.

Secular school and Sunday school teachers need to know that if they say something in a flippant manner that tears down the self-esteem of a young person, they may actually be laying the foundation for a losing wall in the thought processes of that young person.

Parents who fly off the handle and allow negative words to fly out of their mouths need to realize that with every word, they are utilizing the power of the tongue to build walls of limitation and failure in the lives of their own children.

Pastors, youth pastors, and church leaders have to understand that with every negative word that comes out of our mouths, we, too, can be building walls. Sometimes in moments of weakness or anxiety, we reach into our God-given abilities to speak and pull out negatives and hurl them at teenagers who are acting out or causing a disturbance. Those words, although they may seem to have had no affect on the young people at the time, may very well echo in the chambers of their spirits for the rest of their lives. No longer should we stand in our pulpits and declare that a generation is lost, wild, or violent. We should stand in our pulpits and speak positive words because there is too much power locked up inside our tongues, and God's grace is able to redeem the emerging generations. It is high time for us to say so.

The tongue has power, and we have to learn how to use the life that is in that power. When we speak life over the actions and circumstances of our young people and teach then to adopt the same speaking habits, we take great strides in knocking down those retaining walls of failure and loss.

say it louder

Another way to reinforce the winning spirit in young people is to speak well of them publicly—to their parents, their peers, print and electronic media, and the church. Whenever you are speaking to the winners in young people, it's good to do that around other people because the other people make it real in the lives of those teenagers. It is as if the more people hear the positive words, the louder they resonate in the hearts of young people. I love to compliment them both privately and publicly. But for many teenagers, public affirmation just magnifies the compliment and gives them a positive image to live up to.

I love to buy flowers for my wife, Joy. She just loves them. I like to surprise her when I come back from a speaking trip, so I buy her a beautiful bouquet of roses. When she comes home from shopping, she walks into the house and there they are in the privacy of our own home, filling the house with their sweet aroma. She loves that.

But other times I'll bring or send flowers to her music classroom. When my wife gets that bouquet of roses at her job, it is a public display of our private relationship. The other teachers are gathered around the water cooler, and when they see the man coming to deliver the roses, they know the flowers are from me. In doing that publicly, I am actually magnifying the impact of what I am doing. Not only does she know that she is my special love, but all the other teachers, secretaries, janitors, administrators, and students know that Mr. Hill is totally enamored with Mrs. Hill. She is greeted with their coos, catcalls, and playful ribbings.

In all honesty, I am giving her the same bouquets of long-stem roses at home or at work, but the dozens that I give her in public seem to make a greater impact.

When a figure skater finishes a great performance, the audience throws flowers down onto the ice. They could very well just have them delivered to the skater's locker room, but the flowers make a much greater impact when they are shared in public.

Likewise, we need to affirm our teenagers in front of others—even the hard ones. If you have young people who usually are problematic, maybe you need to say to them in a public forum that they are excellent. If they seem to be failing, you need to say to them in a public forum, around their peers, that they are excellent and that they are overcomers. This magnifies the praise and the impact because not only are you willing to speak positively using the power of your tongue over their lives, but you are willing to do so in the presence of other people.

I am reminded of Muhammad Ali. When I was a young African-American male growing up in the sixties and seventies, just a few people (such as Rev. Dr. Martin Luther King Jr. and Minister Malcolm X) had as much impact upon my psyche as Muhammad Ali. Muhammad Ali was such a powerful personage in our urban society that I even owned and played with his action figure. (We didn't call them dolls in my neighborhood; we called them action figures.)

The thing I loved about Muhammad Ali was that he would tell you he was going to whip you and then he would. It was not enough that he would come to the ring with his fists wrapped and ready to kill you. He would come to the ring having already informed you and all your family members of the fact that he was about to whip something on you, and in truth he would try.

Now indeed there were times when he was speaking something I don't think he even firmly believed. I believe there were times that—in the ebonic vernacular—he would be selling wolf tickets; he would be speaking out of the side of his neck. He would be standing there boldly claiming before all the world that he was going to win against someone he was not sure he could defeat. There was something about the confidence this man exuded that made us all believe he could win. It is that type of bold and public "I am the greatest of all time" self-affirmation that magnified the statement. Years later, all over this nation, black men argue over the veracity of Ali's assertion every Saturday morning at the barbershop. That's how loudly that statement was magnified.

anointed to win

David slung his rock and publicly killed Goliath. He did not do it away from the view of people, but he publicly defied the Philistine in front of vast armies.

I believe David knew he would win the battle before he even fought. I believe he was not just trying to psych out Goliath or trying to use some kind of reverse psychology on him. I believe David expected God to step right in the middle of the situation and hand him the win.

This is the critical stage in the development of the winning spirit in the lives of young people. This is the stage when they realize they are anointed to win. This is when they see that God has already called them more than conquerors and that the greater God is inside of them, the lesser gods outside of them. They begin to really believe the Bible and start to actually operate in life as if God was not a man that he should lie.

It is not that they never expect to lose. It is simply that these teenagers expect both their wins and their losses to eventually work out for their personal productivity and developmental good (Romans 8:28).

To some people these kids can appear to be cocky, conceited, or even a little arrogant. But usually they have already climbed over so many mountains of tragedy that it requires a great deal to shake them from their faithful stance of hope and trust in the power and provision of God's grace.

What would appear to be problems and obstacles to other people who have not survived sexual abuse, abandonment, poverty, suicide attempts, drug addiction, or street violence, to these teens are luxuries. In many cases, these teenagers never even dreamed they would still be alive or could have found this much joy, peace, and righteousness in Christ's kingdom (Romans 14:17).

So they have a fresh outlook on problems and begin to embrace challenges as opportunities for God to elevate them either privately or publicly. They already have privately slain their lions and bears, so they are not afraid to lose or win. They are just determined that if they go down, they will have given 100 percent effort and they'll have their shepherds' bags full of stones, ready to fight.

At this final stage they start to apply for colleges they never would have dreamed of even visiting before. They start to think about purchasing homes and starting businesses, finding Christian spouses or living as celibate singles. They begin to exhibit hope and confidence that can make counselors or youth pastors re-examine themselves to see that they are indeed walking in the winning spirit as much as they should.

I am not saying that young people with the winning spirit do not fail and fumble. Yes, they trip, tumble, and sometimes deliberately take a dive. But in most cases, that winning spirit has gripped them so powerfully that losing is no longer comfortable. And their realm of possibilities has been expanded to include this paradigm where they are anointed to win. This place is called *grace*, where God has already given them access to a winning walk, talk, and attitude. Once people have been there, it becomes very difficult for even the most discouraged among them to stay down forever.

A dog will return to his vomit only if he doesn't know there is a steak in his bowl. And the winning spirit teaches young people that they deserve and should expect to have and, therefore, should passionately pursue filet mignon because they are anointed to win.

This is the theme, the catch phrase that I have learned to lace in my sermons. I have emblazoned it on T-shirts and placards and added it to my autograph because when this concept gets way down into the spirit of a young person, it is almost impossible to blast out.

This concept, when coupled with a commitment to daily give 100 percent effort, produces such a marked change in the lives of teenagers that they begin to fall more in love with the gracious Jesus who has called them from the cycle of losing. They also fall more in love with themselves just for having the courage to take the first step out of that cycle and into God's marvelous and amazing grace.

"I am anointed to win," they begin to say, "and even when I lose, I am not rehearsing. I am just researching my next win!"

off with his head

Goliath went down for the count. If I had been David, I probably would have been so shocked that he went down with one shot that I probably would not have reacted with the speed that David did. Perhaps David, not knowing whether Goliath was alive or dead, knew from experience that a wounded predator is even more danger-ous than an uninjured one. He sprang instantly to action, picked up Goliath's sword, and cut off Goliath's head.

The irony of this situation is just wonderful. It's a theme that God, through the vol-umes of the Holy Bible, likes to repeat to us again and again. David used the thing that was designed to destroy him to cut off the head of his enemy. Just as God's grace allowed Samson to use the pillars to which he was chained to kill his captors. Just as God's grace empowered Moses to use the Red Sea that was supposed to drown the children of Israel to drown the legions of Egypt. Just as Jesus used his death on the cross to destroy the works of the devil and redeem lost people back into the good graces of a loving God. The Bible emphasizes this theme to us over and over. We have to teach young people to use the very things that try to kill, steal, or destroy them (John 10:10) to cut off the heads of the same issues that threaten their destiny.

So if they overcame drug abuse and now have the winning spirit, I believe they should be actively involved in ministry that allows them to testify and witness to God's power to liberate others from that painful and self-destructive stronghold. If they were caught in a cycle of losing due to neglect, abandonment, or abuse, I believe they should be trained to return the ministry they have received back to other people who are wrestling with those dark shadows. It doesn't matter if teenagers who now have the winning spirit are leading the class or just making cof-fee and copies. I believe they should be doing something in the ministry that con-tributes to helping cut off the heads of giants.

This is part of the divine justice that seems to help complete healing in the lives of young people who have come out of losing cycles and into a winning spirit. They themselves need to share that spirit with others who are currently losing.

David took what was threatening him and used it to encourage the armies of Israel. David used the weapon of the enemy to decapitate his enemy, and this showed the rest of the Israelite army that God was able to deliver them from the hands of the Philistines, even with their terrible giants.

David cut off Goliath's head. When young people share their testimonies about the grace of God with other young people who are facing those same giants, they cut off the heads of those giants. They drive another nail into the coffins of their own lifestyles of losing, even as they are advertising to other people about God's power to turn losers into winners.

Lets take a minute to look closely at the word *message*.

* God has the power to take the *mess* that was my life and to make me a *message*—a living epistle (letter) to other people who will be able to read me. The focus is not on me; the message is what's important.

- The message is what makes *me* a *sage* to other people.

- Maturity is what gives me the message—*me* and *age*. If I do not commit to keep on growing, I will lose my message.

When raising up young people to walk in newness of life and to live out this winning spirit, we youth workers, pastors, teachers, and parents must actively seek out opportunities for our young people to share how their lives have been impacted by God's empowering grace. In sharing their stories, they not only help encourage their own hearts, but also encourage other young people around them by publicly severing the heads of dead and defeated foes. They make a public spectacle of the issues, problems, or situations that once held them back.

Off with his head! Cutting off the heads of these giants will help to spread the winning spirit. This spirit, this empowering spirit of grace, must be broadcast, shared, translated, and taught if we are to see a new generation arise with a winning spirit (Deuteronomy 28:13).

youth ministry **W**insights

In light of what you have learned in this book, consider your answers to these questions. You may want to discuss these with your youth ministry team.

- Who in your group has conquered a giant?

- What opportunities can you offer for young people to publicly cut off the heads of the giants they have conquered?

- What are you doing in youth ministry that is unnecessary?

- What should you do that you aren't doing right now?

- What visions has God given you for the youth in your group?

- What can you do to help fulfill those visions?

List here a few action steps you'll take to put the message of this book into action in your ministry: